THE ALCHEMIC GLOSARY

FIRST ENCYCLOPEDIC DICTIONARY OF ALCHEMICAL TERMS AND AUTHORS

COMPILED BY:

JOSÉ ANTONIO PUCHE RIART

NOTE: the translation of the Alchemical Glossary from the original Spanish version means that the contents are not all perfectly ordered in the English language.

EDITOR'S FOREWORD (in the first edition, 1979 Juny)

EDICIONES DOBLE-R, FOLLOWING THE EDITORIAL LINE OF PROVIDING THE BEST AND MOST IMPORTANT IN THE FIELD OF IDEAS AND KNOWLEDGE, COULD NOT LEAVE ASIDE THE PUBLICATION OF BOOKS ON ALCHEMY, THE MOST IMPORTANT SUBJECT OF HERMETICISM.

WE BEGIN THE COLLECTION WITH NOTHING LESS THAN THE BOOK BY THE "ILLUMINATED DOCTOR" RAMON LULL, AND CONTINUING WITH THE NEW MEN WHO, GOD WILLING AND PERMITTING, WE WILL ALSO PUBLISH THE LATEST WORK BY THE WELL-KNOWN ALCHEMIST SIMON H.

IN OUR OPINION, THE PRESENT BOOK IS NECESSARY IN THE MARKET, WRITTEN BY A MAN WHO, WE THINK, MAKES AN IMPORTANT CONTRIBUTION TO ALL THOSE SINCERE SEEKERS. J.A. PUCHE R., CIVIL ENGINEER AND WRITER, WILL SURELY SAVE A LOT OF WORK TO THE NEW ALCHEMISTS.

AS A PUBLISHER, I HAVE DECIDED TO INCLUDE HIM AMONG MY WORKS, CONSIDERING HIS IMPORTANT CONTRIBUTIONS TO THE KNOWLEDGE OF ALCHEMY, HIS ARTICLES AND HIS COMMENTARIES ON TEXTS PUBLISHED BY THE TECHNICAL MAGAZINE "QUÍMICA & INDUSTRIA" OF WHICH HE IS A REGULAR CONTRIBUTOR, AND HIS TRANSLATIONS, WHICH HAVE HELPED ME IN THE CHOICE OF THIS BOOK, FOR THIS ESOTERIC COLLECTION OF MY PUBLISHING HOUSE.

THE PUBLISHER, Ramón Rico Sastre

INTRODUCTION (In the first edition, 1979 Juny) by the author,

Jose A. Puche

To date, in our esteemed country, no glossary of alchemical terms worthy of the name has been published, with the honourable exception of the famous treatise "Petit Vademecum d'Alquimia Química" published by Editorial Alta-Fulla in Catalan. However, it is notorious the existence of an abundant and unfinished collection of difficult compilation, scattered among the alchemical texts, placed there by authors of all times, who did not hesitate to leave these scraps of information, clearly so necessary for the study of the classical texts, The use of an aptly whimsical symbology, in order to cover completely all aspects of the elaboration of the Philosophical-Sophical Stone, which to this day remains hidden in the wilds of language, scarcely available to the few scholars knowledgeable in ancient languages, and especially with regard to the words used in Alchemy.

We apologise for any errors or omissions that may have been inadvertently made in the preparation of this text, the work is time-consuming and susceptible to other interpretations, many of which have certainly been left out; the possibility of making further extensions to this Glossary remains open. Nor is it the intention to develop the enormous and complex structure of Alchemy, which many have tried fruitlessly to explain.

I have to thank the Spanish alchemist Simón H. for his contribution to this Glossary, as he has sent forty new words which have been added at the last minute, filling an important "gap" for the lovers of Science.

The creation of this Glossary has as its ultimate aim to be useful to the reader who wishes to carry out research, it makes available information that until now was unpublished in compressed form; the alchemists' book is the support of this varied chemical literature, which conceals beautiful arcana, and is not very accessible given the antiquity of the texts, and the "envy" of the authors of this difficult subject.

INTRODUCTION TO THE ALCHEMICAL GLOSSARY

(In the second edition)

By de author: José A. Puche

As the years go by, life is lived and great experiences are acquired, the point of view necessarily changes and things are discovered that change everything.

With regard to the opening prologue, I am obliged to inform you that not all that glitters is gold, and that the now deceased Simon H. did not have the philosopher's stone he claimed to have. His work with cinnabar enabled him to obtain a corrosive sublimate of high quality, which he pompously called philosophical mercury, and which was the most suitable for the work he taught, the complementary materials being salt and iron sulphate heptahydrate.

The result of the work was a "medicine" which sometimes still contained traces of corrosive sublimate and which had to be removed by heating in the crucible for hours (his salamanders). This medicine had the formula iron hydroxide II, and could be obtained by the dry method by heating pharmaceutical grade iron sulphate II in a crucible and dissolving the croqus obtained in distilled or spring water.

In the course of time I have done other alchemical works, such as the distilled water route, which leads to the "water stone", see the book AGRICULTURA CELESTE", works on the dry path, see the book LA VIA SECA DE LA ALQUIMIA, the KOH and NaOH routes, which we have not published.

The English and French edition of this book is a necessity that some people have suggested to me and this is the occasion to do it. It is February 2021 and 22 years have already passed since I did this work.

The book has its history and I have respected the content exactly, although some influences of the ideas of the best known alchemists at the time I wrote it can be observed.

Nowadays I would not write a glossary, my ideas of alchemy are very different from those I had at the time, and my research objectives have already been fulfilled, the years of work put you in your place and the perspective changes. I see more and more clearly that alchemy and chemistry are becoming one and the same thing passed since I did this work.

THE ALCHEMICAL GLOSSARY

PROLOGUE by the author

This book gives a full account of the most ancient and traditional interpretations of the Art of Alchemy, whose fruits are those of the Tree of Science; not lucubrations laden with outlandish contemplative symbologies replete with sensuality, mysticism and sacredness, it is intended as a defence of the technology involved in this ancient branch of Science, studied pragmatically, with the emphasis on laboratory operations rather than on the anthropological, historical and psychological hobbies to which almost all modern scholars are so fond, sometimes confused by the interpretations of agnostics with their "mental alchemy", which supposedly causes the transmutation of the mind of the individual who practices it, of his life, of his being, and by the school of sexual alchemists, which leads students to the crossroads of epicureanism, plagued by ejaculations, as copious as they are useless, in search of Alchemical Sexuality, Danteanly sanctified at the dawn of ignorance, murkily exploited by the Sons of Cosmic and Divine Orgasms, incapable of understanding the systematic philosophy presented by the classical authors of the Art. Alchemy bears a complementary philosophical burden, which makes its study difficult, even for the most advanced researchers, until its keys are mastered.

The technology of alchemy is uniform throughout the centuries; even when the historical contexts vary, there is a surprising uniformity of multiple coincidences in all the texts of the "Corpus Herméticum", in which all the themes of the Great Work are dealt with exhaustively.

The originality, the content of ideas, the inspiration, the tone, the tenor, the accent, are always present, whatever the source, as far as the "substance" of the words is concerned, universally collected, beyond the sonorous breath transmitted by the vast Hermetic Library, designating to free will the conquest of the golden fleece, absolute of the "chemicals", of Hellenic or Egyptian flavour, once flayed of scholastic, dogmatic, cabalistic and phantasmagoric excrescences, adorned with semantic flourishes, which confuse the most seasoned researcher, illusive argonaut.

As an introduction, I will proceed to give a brief summary of the history of Alchemy, which is already more widely known by contemporary authors, and which can be found in most of the current books on the subject, the only part of Alchemy that was in the public domain until the presentation of this text; to avoid monotony, I will focus on historical exoticism without going any deeper, as I have compiled them anecdotally in my book "The Revolution of the Alchemists", as yet unpublished.

I will begin with the Hebrew people, with the polemical assertion that Genesis and Revelation contain concentrated information on the subject, in spite of future criticism, which undoubtedly proves that both the author of the Pentateuch and St. John were well acquainted with the secrets of Alchemy and Philosophical Elaboration; by virtue of this, the Biblical Patriarchs lived so many years assisted by a high Medicine, which determines the use of the highest grade of Philosopher's Stone by the wet way.

The Egyptians, in the initiatory temples of Isis, kept alight the illustrious flame of Hermetic Knowledge, and the initiates of the Greek mysteries also possessed, as shown in the Aeneid, very extensive knowledge of the phenomena of the chemistry of alchemical "mercury" and of the energetic activation which transforms it into the Philosopher's Stone through the "magnetic" activity inherent in it, when properly treated and kept alive, with the help of God.

The Chinese, in the most remote antiquity, knew of the Island of the Immortals, beings who had such a long life compared to normal people that their eyes became imperishable, this immortality was achieved by ingesting a certain mysterious product that endowed them with eternal youth, a product that we have mentioned in the previous paragraphs.

The Hindus, in texts dating back more than 11,000 years, mention the existence of a certain medicine, SOMA, a beverage obtained from "plants", from which substances capable of curing all illnesses are extracted, as well as giving youth to all people.

The Romans inherited the customs and initiatory schools from the Greeks, until 394, when Emperor Theodosius the Great ordered the closure of all esoteric and hermetic schools in the Empire, even in Egypt. He personally considered these schools to be centres of discord, strombolian and expansive centres that prevented the enslavement of the minds, and which prevented the domination of the perverted Roman court, greedy for wealth and power, seeking slavery based on popular ignorance. This circumstance provoked the subsequent obscurantism in Europe and the loss of all knowledge with the arrival of the barbarians, who encouraged it even more in the face of secular power. With the fall of the gods, Rome collapsed in the following year (395), unprotected from its traditional homelands.

The Arabs inherited technological knowledge from Byzantium, flooded Europe with philosophical, mathematical, alchemical, medical, etc. books, through the Toledo School of translators, filtered the teachings of Geber, Razes, Averroes, Avicenna and many others, illustrating the Middle Ages, which, as Fulcanelli has also shown, was not as "dark" as historians claim, all with the invaluable help of the Temple.

In the Modern Age there are hardly any alchemists, the development of industry and the puritanical and burlesque criticisms of the last and present century have meant that there are very few authors and practitioners of Alchemy, with the exception of our country, France and the USA. At present, Spain is home to the most important School in the world, under the tutelage of Simon H.

Alchemy has fallen into the disrepute of the people, even though in recent years there has been an increase in publications and attraction to this evocative subject, as well as the republication of innumerable ancient texts.

Spain is now aware of the existence of some practising alchemists, whose published works show the extent to which they are achieving positive results. In France, the disappearance of Fulcanelli has been a great loss, for he represented the highest traditional knowledge in that country, and was the last known bastion of the alchemical tradition, to whom I pay my respects.

Today it can safely be said that Spain is the country with the most advanced knowledge in the technology of traditional alchemy, and thus the only bastion in the world with living alchemists at the forefront of these techniques, as effective as they are ancient.

J. A. Puche R, Juny 1979

Post cover:

TO ENRICH AND TRANSFORM MAN IS A TASK THAT MEN OF GENIUS OF ALL TIMES HAVE ATTEMPTED.

ALCHEMISTS, ADVANCED CHARACTERS IN ALL AGES IN TECHNIQUES AND KNOWLEDGE, POSSESS A TOTAL AND INTEGRAL MEDICINE, WITH WHICH THEY MITIGATE THE ILLS OF THEIR FELLOW MEN, IN BODY, SOUL AND SPIRIT.

SPREADING THEIR IDEAS AND THOUGHTS IS, IN OUR OPINION, THE BEST WAY TO HELP IN THE CONSTRUCTION OF THE NEW EARTH, THE NEW HEAVEN, THAT GOD HAS PROMISED US.

THE ALCHEMICAL GLOSSARY FITS PERFECTLY AMONG THE TEXTS OF THE ALCHEMISTS OF ALL TIMES, AND PROVIDES SOLUTIONS TO THE HIEROGLYPHICS THAT HAVE PUZZLED US FOR MANY YEARS.

ABRAHAM THE JEW: A character invented by Nicholas Flamel as the author of the "book" seen in dreams in the "Hieroglyphic Figures".

OIL: In Alchemy it is any viscous liquid with an oily appearance, including among these substances the Universal Medicine.

> **Oil of Sulphur:** For some alchemists it is the "water" that is obtained in the first operation by which the Great Work begins, for which reason it is considered as a "medium substance".

> **Oil of vitriol:** For the latter-day spagyrists it is sulphuric acid, but for the alchemists the name coincides with the "oil of sulphur" and with the "oil of glass" obtained by the reaction of the first substances. The "vitriolus" is the name of the Second Matter.

> **Victory oil:** This is the name given to the fluid obtained in the first reaction of "mercury" with green dyeing sulphur. This is also the name given to the Universal Medicine.

ACID: This coincides with the definition given by chemists, so we will not expand on these matters, which are well known to readers.

STEEL: Irenaeus Philaleteus describes it thus in the Introitus: "Our steel is the flame of our Work, it is the mine of Gold and the whole of the superior and inferior virtues". It is one of the starting principles of Alchemy.

The Cosmopolitan, for his part, reveals that he is in the "womb of Aries", the prime month in which the mercurial "dew" is produced. In the Epilogue he explains that the Pontic water that freezes in the Sun and Moon is obtained from the Sun and Moon by means of the steel of the Philosophers, which is a mutual love of heat and moisture to unite and attract them and their fellows.

The "Steel" turns spontaneously to the "Magnet" and the "Magnet" to the "Steel", in the first reaction of Alchemy, are the hieroglyphics of the first matters.

ACTIVE: Everything that has chemical activity, that acts, that moves, that works within the substance. Also that which lives and can move by itself.

ADEPT: Alchemist who has himself elaborated the Philosopher's Stone.

ADAM: Ancient name of Adam, in Hebrew it means made of red earth, it is the symbol of the alchemical "sulphur", sometimes of the fire of nature, for some it is the symbol of the 3rd Matter, from which the "SALT" is extracted.

ADAMAS, ADAMUS: The same as ADAM.

ADAM: It is the basic matter, united with spirit in the very unity of created substance, immortal and enduring. It coincides with "Adam".

> **Second Adam:** Adam, on leaving paradise, lost his immortal condition, and also his perfection; the alchemist gives this name to the alchemical "Sulphur", a substance very close to gold, although of less density, because of its appearance it has been called "bronze" and "la¬ton", mortal and weak like the 2nd Adam.

ADROP: See AZOTH.

ADMINISTER: To administer a product to provoke a chemical reaction. To administer medicine to a sick person in prescribed doses. To control the use of "water" in the elaboration of the Philosopher's Stone.

AER: In Latin air, volatile element, one of the four natural elements. It is represented as A.

APHRODITE: Also VENUS, is the MOTHER of Eros, the matter from which the first agent is extracted, and also the 2nd Matter of the alchemists.

AGALLA: Mercurial Matter, whose hieroglyph is the OAK, and friend of the ROASTER, which indicates its virility. Analogy that has led the so-called GALENISTS to suppose the GALENA as the first matter of ALCHEMY.

AGENT: FIRST AGENT: Once the ashes have been obtained from the BODY, they will be subjected to CALCINATION, which will burn the heterogeneous and adustible parts, leaving the CENTRAL SALT, our "first agent".

AGRICULTURE: Pseudonym of George Bauer, 16th century alchemist, author of "De re metallica" 1556.

> **Celestial agricultura:** One of the names of Alchemy, because of the similarity of the works of the Art in Agriculture.

AGRIPA, Cornelius: Alchemist, madman and very famous visionary of the 16th century, his works are delirious, surprising and with a reasoned argumentation based on very ancient authors, whom he never understood; it is very pleasant to read his works.

AQUA: WATER: Element, the first product of the Work. It is a very broad term, which refers to the mercurial dew as well as to the mercury of the alchemists, or to the Sophic fire, so that it is convenient to study in each case what is being referred to, according to the meaning that suits it. It is thus represented as V.

In Traditional Alchemy it is the first product that the alchemist obtains at the beginning of his work, and which he will later use throughout the whole work.

Water is obtained by distillation and is used to unite things that are separated. Throughout the whole work, we must not forget that the LIVING WATER gushes forth from the hollow OAK, and with it it drags the SPIRIT, or philosophical "Sulphur". The distillation is iterated several times until the "earth" has been converted into "volatile spirit", rising in the form of white smoke.

> **Aguardiente:** (Aqua ardens). Artefio says: "With our golden water nature is liberated by overcoming nature, and if the bodies are not dissolved by our water, penetrated, diligently ruled, until they abandon their thickness and heaviness, and are changed into a subtle spirit, your

labour will be in vain". This is the product of the first operation. This is also the name given to the specific fire of the alchemists, the spirit which is extracted from the two mineral beginnings; it is the Gate and its key to the Great Work.

Celestial Water: Another name for the first mercury, "fire-water" or simply "water" of the alchemists.

Divine Water: Mercury of the alchemists.

Starry Water: Remember that Fulcanelli, when he speaks of the operation "Revertere et revertar" refers to the star that appears and disappears, the "Star of the Seas", Diana and our "Virgin Mother".

Strong water: Ancient name for nitric acid.

Igneous water: Water of fire, with which the philosophers "burn" by washing. Flamel says "wash in fire, burn with water", it is the first "mercury" of the alchemists.

Mercurial water: First mercury, and also the "Virgin Mother".

Pontic Water: In Latin, "well water", the first solvent, which does not wet the hands, and which is born of the "Chaos" of the sages.

If we study the theses of the "antimonists" such as Eugène Canseliet, we get the following interpretations: It is the "mercury" of the philosophers in its crudest state, before or after the addition of the alchemical catalyst called Ares by Fulcanelli, extracted from the "dew" in the early epoch of Aries, hence the mysterious term "Womb of Aires", "House of Aries", which is considered unintelligible by most of today's readers. The steel of the philosophers is nothing else than a "sulphur" or salt extracted by the retort in successive distillations. This salt, once treated, has the power to dissolve gold.

Mercury, which is not the commercial one, requires the use of these salts throughout the work, as well as the help of the remaining dew, as is pointed out in "rare expe¬riences on the mineral spirit"; this author should not be interpreted literally when he says that: "the mercury must be passed through the skin of a chamois or ram to be cleaned", this expression should be interpreted according to traditional Al-chemy (See Vellocino).

Primitive water: The first solvent, which is also called common "mercury", not to be confused with commercial quicksilver.

Aqua regia: A mixture of nitric and hydrochloric acid, in which metallic GOLD is dissolved, forming gold chloride.

Dry water that does not wet the hands: According to the antimonists, this is the Regulo Martial Star, made of antimony and iron, described by Basil Valentine in the Triumphal Chariot of Antimony, and considered by Canseliet as the alchemical "mercury".

EAGLES: This is the operation that allows us to obtain the first degree of perfection of the Philosophers' Stone, with seven to nine of them the Mercury Regimen is completed and the AZOTH is obtained, with which the Great Work is initiated by the WET PATH, or the Transmutatory Stone is obtained by the DRY PATH. The AZOTH, the double "mercury" of the alchemists, hermaphrodite, is the protagonist throughout the different cycles that it has to undergo, also called Regimes.

The birth of the AZOTH, which takes place under very special conditions, is something marvellous that has never ceased to amaze the alchemists; the light emerges from the darkness in a similar way to the FIAT LUX of Genesis; Following the initiatory teachings, we dare to outline the thesis of the occultists that in order for the LIGHT to manifest on the physical plane, it must manifest on the astral plane, which is achieved by meditation and prayer at the moments of production. As the MUTUS LIBER shows us, the old adage of the monks "ORA ET LABORA" is thus verified as indispensable.

AIR: Any vapour, gas, the atmosphere, one of the four elements, is formed in the interior of the aludel in all Regimes, and serves as a vehicle: "The air has borne it in its bosom".

The alchemical symbol for air is A.

ALAIN DE LILLE: 18th century alchemist, author of "Philosophical Tombstone" 1599.

WINGS: Hieroglyph for the God Mercury, who is very volatile, and symbol of the alchemical mercury or "Universal Di-solvent".

ALEMBIC: Distiller.

> **Alembic of the wise**: The container and the content of the aludel. First materials reacting to obtain water.

ALBIFICATION: See EAGLES.

ALBERT MAGNUS San: 18th century chemist, patron saint of Spanish chemists, author of "Ars Magna".

ALCOTH: Matter before marriage.

ALI-PULI: Alchemist, author of EPISTOLS in 1971.

ALIBORON: Matter useless for Alchemy, or foreign to the Work.

ALIX: Salt.

ALKAEST: Another name for the Mercury of the alchemists, or Universal solvent, as it dissolves any of the products involved in the elaboration of the stone. Fulcanelli calls it "first mercury".

Paracelsus invented this term, which is also applicable to the salts that dissolve gold, even if they are not alchemical.

ALMA: SOUL: Alchemical "sulphur", which appears as a vapour at birth, contained in our water.

ALLEAU, René: French essayist and author of "Aspects of Traditional Alchemy", Editions De Minuit 1953.

ALOSET: Mercury of the Philosophers or AZOTH.

ALMAGRA: This word corresponds to the brass (laton in Spanish). It is interesting to read the fable of Latona in the Aeneid, and in Ovid's Metamorphoses, for its relationship with Alchemy.

ALCHEMY: In ancient times, it encompassed the three sciences of Alchemy, Spagyrics and Chemistry.

Nowadays, it is advisable to separate these three sciences, as they have become increasingly distant in terms of procedures, ideas and spiritual or metaphysical approaches.

Alchemy has been practised, as always, by an elite of people, brilliant in mentality and spirituality; those who have not given "the key" have not been admitted into the bosom of the "adepts" (people who have obtained the Philosopher's Stone). They have always brought about a revolution in the knowledge of the other sciences throughout history, with their scientific contributions, and their more heterodox and profound points of view.

Spagyrics has its mineralistic branches, whose aim is metallic transmutation and metal medicines. It is related to Alchemy because they use the 2nd matter as an element capable of initiating transmutations; the vegetalist branches seek to obtain drugs or poisons from the vegetable kingdom, and remain related to the apothecaries at present, as their objectives coincide.

ALCHEMIST: A person who practices Alchemy or Spagyrics.

ALCHEMIST ANONYMOUS GERMAN: Pseudonym of Limojon de S. Didier, author of the "Hermetic Triumph" and "The Knights' War".

ALTINORAUM: Vitriol, the living "Gold" of the Alchemists.

ALTUS: Pseudonym of Jacob Sulat, author of the Mutus Liber, published by Luis Cárcamo in a replica of the 1672 edition, annotated by E. Canseliet. Also published by Muñoz Moya without commentary.

ALUDEL or ALUTEL: Vessel necessary for the Great Work. Sublimator.

AMALGAMA: A mixture of two metals, intimately united by fusion. In antimonist Alchemy it refers to the preparation of mercury albified by the Eagles with gold, preparing it for the Great Firing, the final phase of the Great Work.

In traditional Alchemy, it is the mixture of "Salt", "Sulphur" and "Mercury", mixed in the correct proportion to perform the "sublimations".

AMMONIAC - AMMONIACO: See Harmoniac. Ammonium nitrate ($NH2 - NO3$)

AMATEUR OF SCIENCE: Amateur who studies Al-chemy without doing laboratory work, only at a theoretical level.

ANA: Addition of two salts to parts of equal weight. The Mother of the Mother in Mine¬ral Theology, as Ana is the Mother of the Virgin Mary.

ANCIAN: Used in Alchemy to point to the Father of the Metals, Saturn, who devours his children. It points to the lead of the Philosophers and the mercury of the alchemists. It is the faithful servant, the pilgrim and travelling mercury that is obtained from a common substance, available to all, and which takes the form of a mysterious water.

ANCHLA: Marine symbol used to designate the philosophical sulphur, which anchors the mythical island of Delos, the only one of the Hermetic Sea.

ANDRADE Valentin: Author of the Chemical Wedding of Kristian Rosenkreutz, 1469, published by the Esoteric Library, Ed. 7 ½.

ANDRODUNOS: See ANDROGINO.

ANDROGINO: The "mercury of the philosophers" is usually so designated, and is elaborated and whitened, obtained from the union of man (in Greek Andros) and woman (in Greek Ginos). The Aniamated Mercury possesses the two principles in its body, the Sulphur, which in its successive battles has been dissolving into Mercury, and has been communicating to it its special characteristics. This "mercury" is called Hermaphrodite, Androdunos, Milk of the Virgin, etc., by the ancient authors, the male and female having been blended in one body. It is the AZOTH.

ANERIT: Living or animated sulphur.

ANIADUN: Graces that the Holy Spirit infuses.

ANIMAR: To infuse the soul. To give life to a compound.

ANTIMONIUM: Metal that the "antimonists" confuse with the "mercury" of the alchemists. It is obtained from Kermes or Stibnite. It has been the subject of studies by Basil Valentine, who explains how the "stone of fire" can be obtained from it, similar to the philosopher's stone in its properties, but far removed from its nature.

In Alchemy it is often used to hide the subject of the sages from the eyes of the vulgar, and as Fulcanelli rightly says, nothing could be further from the Great Work.

ANTIMONIST: An alchemist who works with antimony to try to obtain the Philosophical Stone. It is well known that antimonists have never achieved useful results in their work, as is the case with Eugene Canseliet and his followers.

ANTHONY, St.: Hieroglyph of Antimony in Catholic Mineral Theophany.

AQUIN, St. Thomas: Theologian, philosopher, alchemist, disciple of Albert the Great and author of numerous texts on alchemy, as well as being one of the "Fathers of the Church".

ARACELI: Literally "Celestial Stone", Philosopher's Stone, marvellous Elixir, Universal Medicine, Panacea that cures all ills.

SPIDER: Iron and MAGNET, the rising SUN, the EAST.

TREE: The Solar Tree, the Tree of Science of the Earthly Paradise, the Tree of Set and of Victory, which according to Mosaic tradition will rebound in manifestation against the forces of the Dark Ages. In Hebrew Set means tumults, ruins and foundation. The dry Tree is the hieroglyphic of the dead metals, from the point of view of Alchemy. It is able to rejuvenate and give them life by the operation of "re-incrudation".

The TREE is the alchemical hieroglyph that serves to express metallic inertia, the state in which human industry places metals after reducing and melting them.

The dry TREE is also the hieroglyph for Sulphur, being devoid of foliage and reduced to its skeleton.

ARK: Hermetically sealed vessel containing the compound, rebis or anagram.

ARCANE: Secret, occult, complete alchemical procedure not revealed, which describes a Regimen or fraction of it.

> **Major Arcanum:** This is the knowledge of the materials from which SALT, SULPHUR and MERCURY are born, namely the "body", the "soul" and the "spirit" of the Great Work. They also imply the complete knowledge of the process of the Great Work.

ARES: Iron, Mars, also designates the IMAN, the 2nd matter of the Great Work, from which the "soul" of the world is extracted.

ARFE: Burnt, burnt, sometimes designates the Raven or Sulphur by the black colour of the soot. It comes from the Latin Arfus. Alchemical synonym of the Raven.

ARGENTUM VIVUM: In spagyrics it refers to the mercurous metal (Hydrargirium) Hg. or quicksilver used by glassmakers in the manufacture of mirrors, extracted in Almadén. In Alchemy it is used to indicate the mysterious alchemical "mercury" in any phase of the execution of the Great Work.

ARGOT: Language used by alchemists to understand each other. According to Fulcanelli it designates the Gothic and Gothic Art of alchemical and philosophical dwellings and constructions, such as Notre Dame. See Kabbalah.

ARIANA: The mythical thread of Ariana allowed Theseus to escape from the Palace of the Minotaur. In Alchemy this expression is used to explain the correct development throughout the Mercury Regime, especially when performing the sublimations. See ARAÑA.

ARIES: Spring month, beginning at the vernal equinox, nature is awakened, all the plants blossom and sprout their seed, the dew brings its infinitesimal quantities of elements which fertilise the earth.

HARMONIACO, Salt: According to the thesis of the antimonists, it is the "ana" addition of the two salts obtained from the dew; it has the property of communicating a great acrimony to the Starry Martial Regulus. It is so called because it is the only salt that acts as a mediator and puts Sulphur and Mercury in "harmony" in the Eagles, to compose the Animated Mercury; it is obtained from the tartar of the barrels.

ERMINE: AZOTH, philosophical mercury of the su¬bli¬mations.

ARNALDO DE VILANOVA: 13th century Mallorcan doctor, alchemist, renowned spagyrist, author of numerous books on alchemy, in which he studies the transmutation of metals by hermetic and spagyrical procedures known as "parti¬cular". He is the author of the "New Light of the Chemists", "The Great Rosary", "The Treasury of the The-soros", "The Flower of the Flowers", "Aspects of Alchemy", etc. The original works can still be read in Latin in the National Library in Madrid, as well as some translated copies, in "Libros Ra¬ros" (Researchers' Room).

ARCHEO: In general this word refers to the Dew, as a spirit or mineral vapour that is everywhere, does not belong to any of the three kingdoms of nature (animal, vegetable, mineral), and is the driving spirit of the world and of the Great Work, with the power to fertilise and ferment. It is the alchemical "mercury".

ARSENIC: The name Arsenic, the lesser moon of the spagyrics, is usually given to alchemical sulphur in the oldest treatises; it comes from the Greek ARSENIKON, which translates as "manly, virile". The confusion with the dangerous metal has caused quite a few poisonings in the past, just as it happened with lead and mercury, when the very toxic vapours were inhaled, without due precautions, when released by the furnace fire.

    Yellow arsenic: Philosophical sulphur.

    Arsenic, Red: Philosophers' salt.

ART, Great: Name of Alchemy.

ARTEFIO: Alchemist and author of the 12th century, wrote marvellous works on alchemy, among them "The Secret Book", including his translation of the work of Lapidus, "The Treatise on the Philosopher's Stone" 1612.

ARTEMISA: Daughter of Zeus and Latona, sister of Apollo, she is also known as Diana, white stone.

ASS: Lucius Apuleius, in the "Golden Ass" treats the 2nd matter of the Great Work in this way.

ASTRE: From "Astre", shining, glittering.

ATANOR: Oven of Alchemy, in which the vessels are placed to maintain them at the temperatures required by the Art. Atanor comes from Athanatos, immortal, because the fire must never be extinguished.

Nowadays, the charcoal oven has been replaced by GAS burners, for reasons of hygiene and comfort, and without diminishing the quality of the Philosopher's Stone obtained, but electronic energy sources should not be used, as some authors say.

ATANOR is also understood to be the prepared substances which serve as a covering for the central nucleus where the latent faculties, which the fire will activate, slumber.

AURUM: May be interpreted as the multiplication through the Turning of the Wheel, or repetition of the processes from and including the Mercury Regime, so that the stone, in each of the turns or interactions, multiplies its potency tenfold, both in the DRY and WET ways.

> **Aurum albeum:** This is the name generally given to the animated Mercury obtained in the Lunar Regime, and to the White Philosopher's Stone, useful for obtaining silver by

transmutation, or for Medicine, depending on whether or not it is "oriented".

Aurum potabilis: Another name for Universal Medicine.

AVALLON: Island of Atlantis, also known as the Island of the Apple Trees, where the "Golden Apples" were bred, on which Hercules relied in one of his mysterious Journeys to confer Immortality.

The alchemists emphasise that this White Island or Remora, like the one on which Apollo (Solar God) rules, coincides with the centre of the Earth of which so many alchemists speak, the Land of the Grail, AND the Isle of Glass. It is represented by the cross, similar to the Na¬zi, but with the blades turning in the opposite direction, due to the rotation it takes in the mysterious solution of Sulphur in Mercury.

BIRD OF HERMES: A volatile bird that sacrifices itself to obtain the Philosophical Mercury. This name corresponds to the simple white mercury.

AZOGUE: Mercury metal (Hg). It was used for the azoguing of mirrors, but in alchemy this is the name given to the mercury of the alchemists. Nowadays, the use of the liquid metal is widespread in industry, from its use in thermal and atomic power stations, to the manufacture of explosives, thermometers, measurements, etc.

AZOTH: Name of the alchemical Double Mercury. It comprises the first and last letters of the Greek, Latin and Hebrew alphabets, symbolising "from the beginning to the end of all the universe", the letter H symbolises the sun H = Helios (Sun), symbol of the Great Work; this product is born in each sublimation and is the only protagonist of our work.

SULPHUR: In spagyrics it is one of the parts that make up the metals, sulphur and mercury that make up the metal according to the proportion of each one. According to Canseliet, it is the product derived from the Caput Mortuum obtained in the manufacture of the Regulus, either by means of the long wet process of forty days, or with the appropriate catalyst for the dry process in the cri-sol and in a short time.

In Alchemy, SULPHUR is the name of the dissolved metal extracted by the solvent; it is the PRINCIPE, the seed of the dead metal which feeds on the nutritive elements of the Mercury, with which it evolves, killing the living metallic water and thus giving birth to the metallic SULPHUR, which is ALIVE and which will unite with life through the well-known CHEMICAL WEDDING.

DRAGON SLIME: Foam floating on the "hermetic sea", which is carefully collected so that it does not go up in smoke, has a greasy appearance, a blackish colour and a cadaverous smell. This oil is a sign of dissolution.

BACO: God of wine, who in alchemy is a simile of the Wine of the Philosophers and the mercury of the wise men. He has also been called Evius.

BACON, Roger: Alchemist and philosopher, 13th century British Franciscan monk, author of "The Root of the World" (Radix mundii). He was one of the most brilliant minds of his time, and a great philosopher.

BAFOMET: Templar symbol which contains the secrets of the manufacture of the Philosophical Stone, and which contains the Traditions of the Baptism of Methe or solar initiation.

BALNEUM MARIAE - BATH OF MARY: This is a hot water bath in which the vessel is placed as if it were in the sea. It is used for gentle distillations, avoiding direct contact between the flame and the distilling vessel.

Due to the particular conditions of this type of distillation, it is also known as Vientre Equino or Vientre de caballo, horse dung due to the working temperature of the furnace, and Baño María, as it is presumed that it was discovered by Mary the Jewess, sister of Moses, to whom a treatise on Hermetic Philosophy is attributed. It is also called FONS FILOSOFARUM.

The vessel introduced into the SEA BATH is bathed as in the sea. The water that bathes the vessel is replaced as it evaporates by other hot water.

Some alchemists use the bath with thermostat and independent heating circuit, proving the system to be very practical.

The applications of the BATH OF MARY are mainly distillations and putrefactions.

KING'S BATH: The preparation of the REBIS to undergo the cooking corresponding to the Regime of Sa¬turno, as explained by Bernardo de Treves, Count of the Marca Trevisana in "La Palabra Abandona¬da" (The Abandoned Word).

The antimonists give a very clumsy explanation, supposing that it is the mixture of gold metal with antimony treated by the procedure described by Canseliet as "sublimations", and they have invented the "chromatic range" which runs through the compound.

BARBAULT, René: He is a French alchemist and astrologer, currently alive, author of "L'Or du millième Matín", Publications Prèmièrs, Paris. His family constantly helps him in his spagyric works. This book has been published in Castilian and is currently on sale.

BASIL VALENTIN: Pseudonym of Senior Zadhit, who passed himself off as a Benedictine monk and adept in the 15th century, although his lexicon is from the following century. The pseudonym is broken down into two others: Basileos and Valentin, a brave friend of truth. In Spain, all his works are available in the Biblioteca Nacional, as they have been translated. The most important are: Triumphal chariot of antimonius, (Luis Carcamo Ed.), Triumphal chariot of antiminius (Plaza y Janes Ed.), Azoth treatise, (there is a translation of the second part, made by Julio Peradejordi, and another complete one that has been deposited in the National Library), The Twelve Keys to Philosophy (Miguel Ángel Muñoz Moya editores).

BASILIS: Mythological animal, used by the alchemists to hide the metallic SULPHUR, our hermetic SUN.

STICK: Rod of Hermes, Caduceus, attribute of Mercury.

BEETLE: Fruit of the OAK, which is the symbol of the 1st Matter.

BERGIER, Jacques: Contemporary essayist, author of "The Witches' Rebellion" and "The Return of the Witches". He hardly mentions the subject of Alchemy.

BERIGARDO DE PISA: Italian alchemist of the 17th century.

BERNARD OF TREVES: Count of the Marca Trevisana: This alchemist has been well known since the 15th century. His works, pure allegory, are highly appreciated by alchemists for their remarkable clarity. The most important are: "The Abandoned Word" (Ed. 7 1/2), "A Treatise on the Philosophy of Metals" (Ed. 7 1/2 and Salmon VolII) and "The Treatise on the Egg of the Philosophers", which I have translated myself.

BERNARD OF TREVES: French alchemist of the 17th century, of the same name as the previous one.

BETHEL: Derived from the Greek Baitulos, a stone that fell from heaven and was given to Adam in Paradise; in Hebrew it means House of the King, house of the Lord. According to Genesis (XVIII-11 and 12) Jacob, the conqueror of the Angel, gave the name Bethel to the terrible place that marked the point where a stairway joined Heaven and Earth, which inspired Altus to create the first plate of the Mutus Liber.

"How dreadful is this place, this place is none other than the House of God and it is the Gate of Heaven. The ladder is the mediator or intermediary between Heaven and Earth. It rests on the black stone, the Bethel.

In Genesis (XXVIII-36 and XXXIII-25, 31 and 32), we read:

"I will no longer call you JACOB for you fought against Elohim and men, and overcame them".

Seth took a branch of the plant of Paradise, thus conquering the Grail. The black colour of the Kaaba Stone points to that of the initial CHAOS, the mysterious OAK.

In Basil Valentine's Treatise on the Azoth, Saturn, crowned at the apex of a drawing representing the Great Work, has the symbol of sulphur beneath him, complementing the hieroglyphic.

In the initiatory Rites of the Religion of the Mysteries, the Bethel is the House of the God Bread, the house of Ceres, God of Roman times.

CAPILLARY WHITENING: The very white colour which the Work takes on during the Lunar Regime; the compound takes on the appearance of fine threads from the periphery towards the centre, the white colour beginning on the surface and gradually reaching the heart of the vessel as the Regime progresses.

CHEMICAL WEDDINGS: Action with which the Mercury Regimen is completed, in which the BODY, the SOUL and the SPIRIT are united, namely SALT, SULPHUR and MERCURY, respectively, obtaining AZOTH, the only substance with which the Philosopher's Stone can be obtained.

The Chemical Wedding is therefore another name given to the SUBLIMATIONS or EAGLES, in which the first mercury is united to the living "Sulphur", thus obtaining the MERCURY of the PHILOSOPHOS or DOUBLE MERCURY.

BOHAS: One of the columns of the Temple of Solomon.

BÖTTGER, Johann Friedrich: A deceitful spagyricon who tried to deceive the Elector of Saxony; the latter had him imprisoned for claiming to know the Stone in all the details of its elaboration; he regained the favours of H.M. by discovering the Saxon porcelain, from Kaolin, from which they obtained substantial profits.

BRETON, Le: Well-known French alchemist of the 18th century, author of "Les Clés de la Philososphie Espagirique", Jombert, 1722.

BOYLE, Robert: 17th century physicist and chemist, who established the Law with his name in Chemistry, lover of the Science of Hermes and witness of numerous metallic transmutations.

BRONZE: In Alchemy it is the most hidden symbol of sulphur, in its reference to copper and brass. It also designates metallic gold; in Spagyric it designates the alloy known in industry as bronze.

BUCHARDT, Titus: Author of "Alchemy" (Plaza y Janés Ed). He is a contemporary technician of the French ve¬cina.

BEST KNOWN ALCHEMY LIBRARIES:

- Library of the Chemical Philosophers, J.J. Manguet.

- Biblioteca Chemica Curiosa.

- Teatrum Chemicum Britanicum. The best compilation by Elias Ashmole, 1652.

- Musaeum Herméticum.

CABALA: The most hidden meaning is that of tradition, the key to Science. It comes from the Latin Cabalus, horse or mare that bears the weight of knowledge enclosed in Tradition. Not to be confused with the famous Hebraic Kabbala for interpreting the Bible and other ancient Jewish texts. There is also "phonetic Kabbalah", in which words with a similar "sound" are used to conceal others, and this is the technique favoured by Fulcanelli in his language, French.

HORSE OF THE SUN: Not suitable for the Work.

HORSE HEADS: Symbol of the colour black, which appears when the work is carried out on various occasions, receiving the name of mortification and putrefaction:

- When obtaining the common "mercury" of the alchemists.

- At the birth of the Hermetic REBIS.

- During the Regime of Saturn.

CHAIN: French hieroglyph of the 1st Matter.

CADUCEUS: Mercury's rod on which a snake and a serpent are coiled, as a symbol of peace and reconciliation.

Mercury is the herald or heraldess of the Work, and the CADUCEO has this meaning.

CAIN: First son of Adam, who in Alchemy is the 2nd Matter. Cain means Acquisition, and the first thing obtained is a NEGRA substance, the Raven, also called the BLACK AND RABIOUS DOG, the first witness of the Magisterium.

LIME: Any product that is presented in powder form, among which lime can be included.

CALCINATE: This word has many meanings in Alchemy and Spagyrics, of which it is worth mentioning:

- It is the pulverisation by crushing of any solid body, until it is converted into a "lime" of very small fragments.

- Spagyric calcination consists of applying temperature in a furnace or athanor to dry a body by the action of fire, in order to deprive it of its radical humidity and obtain its ashes in the form of powder.

- Other spagyrics consider calcination to be based on supplying a strong acid that corrodes the product, reducing it to powder.

- Another interpretation is the reduction by means of a non-burning ca¬lor, as occurs in obtaining the second salt of the dew, in a bain-marie, according to Canseliet's thesis.

CALCINATION: Operation by which matter is subjected to the action of flame, without melting, and is reduced to ashes, showing its salt.

CALID King: Famous sultan or caliph whose existence has not been proven, to whom beautiful treatises on alchemy are attributed, to which he "was" fond of.

HEAT: Indicates the temperature at which cooking is carried out. The heat is regulated by the different "degrees of fire".

NATURAL HEAT: In the past, when they spoke of this heat, they generally referred to the nature of the material they were studying, according to the appearance it presented to the senses.

Alchemists call one of the raw materials of the Great Work by this name.

BED: The place where the philosophical vessel sits within the athanor. Support of the alchemical material.

CHAMELEON: The AZOTH, as it discovers the different regimes, takes on all the colours of the spectrum, which denote the chromatic character of the chameleon.

FIELD: Alchemist's Laboratory, the place where the philosopher's seed or vessel is poured, the collection point of the dew in the countryside. Alchemical amalgam prepared for the collection of the mercurial harvest (CHAOS).

LAURENTINO FIELD: Field of grafted gold.

CANSELIET, Eugène: Contemporary French antimonist alchemist, recently deceased, supposed disciple of Fulcanelli, author of numerous works on alchemy, of which the following deserve special mention:

- "Two Alchemical Lodges", Schemit 1946, Paris.

- "Alchemy", L.L Pauvert 1964, Paris.

- "The alchemy explained on classical texts", Luis Carcamo, Madrid.

- "The Twelve Keys of Philosophy", commented by him (the work is by Basilio Valentín), and translated by Muñoz Moya, who published it in 1987.

- "The Mutus Liber" comments, Luis Cárcamo editor.

This author became famous because the Government of the neighbouring French nation begged him not to manufacture gold in abundant quantities so that the prices of the coveted metal would not fall; although he never achieved the transmutation.

Fulcanelli and Canseliet hold totally different doctrines, which must be emphasised against the second alchemist.

CHAOS: The first mineral matter is called chaos by the philosophers, for it is from chaos that the whole alchemical nature develops.

It is the ANCIENT, the father of metals.

It is the FIRST MERCURY, obtained under the "drying action" of arsenical "sulphur", embodied, it takes the form of a solid, black, dense, fibrous, brittle and friable mass, called SECOND CHAOS, common mercury or spirit, it is our solvent.

CAPARROSE (BLUE): Copper sulphate, light blue in colour.

CAPARROSE (GREEN): Iron sulphate, green in colour, similar to Cardenillo (cupper carbonate).

CAPRICORN: It is a sign of the zodiac in which the Sun enters on the 22nd of December, the day of the winter solstice. Some avaricious alchemists use it as a hieroglyphic of Aries, confusing the goat with the ram, since spring is of great importance in Alchemy, and the energy of the SUN manifests itself with great force, its VIVIFICANT power being at its maximum, necessary in certain phases of the Work.

CAPILLARY: From the Latin capillaris, designating a very thin tube in relation to its length. Flamel uses the expression "capillary circle" in the sense of wheel fire, with which he designates Mercury.

See "Capillary Whiteness".

CAPUT MORTUUM: Literally: Dead Head.

It is the condemned earth of the BODY, impure, inert, sterile, which the solvent with its action separates, precipitates and rejects as a useless and worthless residue.

For antimonists, it is the black residue that remains after obtaining the Star Martial Regulus.

CARBUNCLE: Completely finished Philosopher's Stone. Universal medicine.

CARITATIVE: Expression that points to the alchemist who clearly explains some part of Alchemy. The information is abundant; all parts of the Great Work have been exhaustively written about, but in bits and pieces, and confusing some parts with others, in order to keep away those who are not particularly interested, and who have the patience to unravel the intricate web of Ariana's Thread, so skilfully prepared.

Charity consists in clearing up some of the unknowns in an unvarnished way. Charity = clarity of explanation and no deception. As an example of charitable books, we should cite the works of Simon H: "The Golden Book of Alchemy", "The Doves of Diana" or also "The Closed Door", in which they say just enough, very little but everything is true.

As for procedural charitables, the author of the "Rosary of Philosophies" and the author of "Metaphysical-Cabbalistic-Hermetic Concordances" are cited.

CARO, Roger: Contemporary French alchemist, author of "Concordances Alchimistes", 1968. Books can be purchased at his home address: Chemin de la Madrague nº 83. St. Cyr - Sur - Mer. France.

CATHOLIC: From the Greek Catolikos - ke - kon, which means universal, according to the rules of the Hermetic Tradition, this qualifier is extended to ALKAEST, universal solvent in Alchemy.

CATHOLICON: Medicine of the Sages, the main objective of the alchemists.

PRIMING: Action by which the necessary humidity is supplied to the Philosopher's Stone so that it can carry out a complete Regimen, under the watchful eye of the alchemist.

The antimonists call priming the operation of moistening their antimony little by little, by means of two or three small irrigations, in order to prepare the compound for its "sublimations", as useless as they are laborious.

CENTRE OF THE EARTH: It is the mysterious violet island floating in the centre of the alchemical ocean, enclosed in the vessel, which appears in the preparation of sulphur during the stormy and philosophical firing of the sand fire. It also appears in the firing of the galena regula, in the second phase of the galenists.

RED WAX: Philosopher's stone of transmutation, obtained by wet process, it is very fusible, it melts at 64ºC according to Fulcanelli.

CETRUS: Rod of Mercury, alchemical "mercury".

Sceptre of the Mad Mother: Alchemical sulphur.

HEAVEN OF THE PHILOSOPHERS: Alchemical Mercury, in the phases in which the "North Star" appears, similar to that of antimony.

CINABRIUM: In alchemy it designates a certain dark red product, very similar in appearance to the crystals of the sulphide of mercury (cinnabar), the stone of the wet way.

KINOPHALUS: Dog's head. Tot, Egyptian god, Greek Hermes and Latin Mercury.

CIRCULAR: It is a distillation in which the liquid that is distilled falls back into the vessel, so that it travels a closed circuit that some authors call the Circle of Nature; the fluid does a continuous work in perpetual movement, capable of astonishing the primitive chemists, and was used to concentrate the essences of the pharmacists. Today it is known as LIXIVATION in chemistry.

The word comes from the Latin Circueo and Circumeo.

In Alchemy also the natural circulation corresponds to the Fire of the Wheel, in the elaboration of the Philosopher's Stone. The stone is redissolved in Mercury, to make the Eagles again.

SWAN: Volatile, which by its wings is assimilated to Mercury.

White Swan: AZOTH, double or philosophical Mercury.

philosophical.

Roasted Swan: The same.

CLEF DU GABINET HERMETIQUE: 18th century manuscript.

COAGULAR: From the Latin coagulare, to curdle, indicating the passage from the liquid to the solid state.

Geber in the Summa (Ch. 5 book 1) explains that it is the reduction of a fluid to a solid by the privation of its water.

The Spagyricon recognises four methods of curdling: cooling, evaporation, heat by keeping at a constant temperature in a closed container, as occurs in the preparation of hard-boiled eggs.

COPPER: Its planet is Venus, its Greek name is Kupros, pointing to "sulphur" in Greek Sonfros, by phonetic-cabalistic analogy.

The Régime of Venus in Alchemy follows that of the Moon in the Great Work. It is characterised by the colours of the Peacock's tail.

The most common hieroglyph used by alchemists to hide "sulphur" is precisely that of copper or brass.

The hieroglyph of Venus, which, when weathered, is greenish in colour, hides precisely that of the second matter of the Great Work, our first Adam.

COOKING: Said in Spagyric terms, it is the presence of any matter in the athanor, exposed to the flame, or to the heat of gases, or to the reverberated fire, or to the bath of Mary, or in the chapel of the tower, as long as boiling is not produced.

In alchemical terms, it is the process to which the Rebis undergoes, throughout the Regimes of Alchemy, until the most complete maturation of the Stone.

CODICIOUS: Alchemist who deceives the neophyte in order to lead him away from obtaining the Stone, teaches false things that ruin the work of the one who begins it and is not capable of separating the chaff from the grain.

COHOBATION: Distillation with "circulation" for the purpose of concentrating a product. It is perfectly described in Lemery's Treatise on Chemistry. Leaching. See Circular.

Peacock'S TAIL: During the execution of the Venus regime, all the colours of a male peacock's tail appear, so characteristic of the male peacock that they will cease on reaching the Mars regime.

COLOURS OF THE GREAT ALCHEMICAL WORK: The colours which appear in the different phases of the Ela¬bo¬ration are emblematic of the various substances and regimes in which they appear or intervene.

Black: This is the colour of Saturn, the emblem of the Lead of the Philosophers, the black dragon. It is the colour of Chaos or first matter. It is also the colour of death, of the Raven and of Putrefaction, emblem of the alchemical Sulphur.

White: It is the colour of Purity, of sublimated Mercury, indicating Light. The Chaldeans with the voice "hur-heurim" indicated the white, the pure, the noble. White is the colour of the White Stone, which transmutes metals into pure Silver. It is the colour of the Lunar Regime.

Red: It is the colour of fire, of exaltation by the Sophic fire, of the Red Stone which transmutes all metals into gold. On the other hand, it is the symbol of volatility, the predominance of spirit over matter; it is the hieroglyphic of the Sophic fire obtained from the spring spirit that floods the fields in the morning. It is the colour of the Solar Regime

Blue: The colour of Venus, the colour of the earth when it replaces black, the symbol of copper, emblematic of alchemical sulphur.

Green: It is the colour of water, and also of the 2nd matter of the Great Work. It appears in the Venus Regime.

Citrine: Colour of the Regime of Mars.

Grey: Emblematic colour of St. Christopher, bearer of Gold, and characteristic of the Regime of Jupiter, third of the Great Work.

HIVE: Symbol used by Fulcanelli to indicate the 1st Matter of the Work or metallic Chaos.

COMBAT: Reaction of two matters in different phases of the Work. (1st conjunction, eagles, etc).

COMBUSTION: Action of fire on matter, which combines with atmospheric phlogiston (oxygen). An excess of fire burns the alchemical "phlogiston", destroying the work by producing the dreaded reddish precipitate, which indicates the premature death of the compound due to excess heat in the aludel.

ALCHEMICAL FUEL: That of the eternal lamps described by Fulcanelli.

COMPOUND: The contents of the vessel, at any point in the Great Work.

CONCH: Fulcanelli uses it as a symbol of the Alchemical Mercury, or Blessed Water.

FREEZE: See coagulate.

CONFECTION: from the Latin confectio, coincides with composition or compound.

CONGREGATION: From the Latin congregatio, meeting, assembly, board, society, "mob". Mixture. Assembly.

CONJUNCTION: Chemical act by which two or more substances are transformed into another substance that combines them.

COPELATION: Test discovered by Geber to test gold with ashes, in this test only the gold remains and the other metals disappear. There is always a loss of the noble metal, and it is nowadays the supreme test for gold. The procedure can be read in more detail in the Mantisa Metallurgica written by Theophilus (Bibliotheca Nazionale, Introduction to the Introitus of Irenaeus Philaleteus by Theophilus).

COPULA: Action of union of the male and female. In alchemy it coincides with conjunction, the union of two chemical compounds.

CORNUDA: French idiom that is equivalent to "re¬torta", generally coming from a bad translation, or from a desire to make the translation more obscure.

The name comes from the horn-like arm on these devices.

COSMOPOLITE, The: Pseudonym of Alexander Sheton, 16th century adept, author of the "New Light of the Chemists", Paris 1723, and of the "Philosophical Letter" (Vision Books).

Raven: Black colour that appears at different moments in the work, namely in the 1st conjunction, sublimations, Jupiter's Regime, etc.

CRANEUS: From Kraios (head, what it sees), the culminating point of the work.

CRYPT: From the Greek Kriptos, hidden, in which the secrets of the Hermetic tradition are kept, such as the statuettes of Isis and Saint Anne.

CHRISTOPHER (Saint): The alchemical legend of Saint Christopher is of great value, we can read it in the books of Fulcanelli; the name of the saint comes from the Greek Chrysophoros, he who carries the gold, he is the hieroglyph of sulphur in the Mineral Theophany, he is the Rising Gold of Alchemy, and his emblematic colour is grey, just as for Mercury it is violet.

CRISOL: An earthenware or porcelain utensil similar in shape to a cup in which the material to be operated on by the dry method is placed. It comes from the Latin Crucibulum and is represented by a cross.

CRISOPEYA: This word is composed of the Greek words chrysos, gold, and poeios, manufacture. The most literal translation is the technique of making gold. The most common translation is the making of the philosopher's stone. The chrysopeia also includes the particular spagyric procedures, which are very close to alchemy, as they always touch one of the most important points, the 2nd dispensing matter of the DYE.

CROSS: It is the symbol that represents the crucible in Alchemy and Spagyrics. In Mineral Theophany, the three nails are the image of the three pu¬rifications by fire.

The crucible is only used for the orientation of medicine to gold in Alchemy. The theophanic translation of the INRI is: Ignis Natura Renovatur Integra, Nature is renewed in its entirety by Fire.

CUBE: It is the symbol of the Philosopher's Stone, a cubic stone with six faces, and of the six regimes of the Fire of the Wheel, which indicate the rotation of the very secret "Centre of the Earth" around its "axis".

CUCURBIT: Retort.

BODY: It is the principle of fixity, the "blue", which possesses the property of depriving the other principles of their volatility. It retains the Soul and the spirit in such a way that they can no longer be separated.

CYLIANI: Unknown alchemist of the 19th century, who signed himself Cy., and who in the later editions of "Hermes Unveiled" appears under the full pseudonym. Cyliani opens wide the door to the alchemical labyrinth with his work, translated into Spanish and published by Luis Cárcamo in Algora Corbi's "Tabla Redonda de los Alquimistas".

CHAMPAGNE, Jean Julien: Illustrator of Fulcanelli's works, died in 1932. Some authors know that he was really the master who hid behind the pseudonym Fulcanelli, nowadays it is impossible to determine if he really was, as all those who knew who Fulcanelli really was have died.

CHEVALIER INCONUE: Author of "La Nature au decouvert", Aix, 1669.

DANAE AND PERSEUS: Legend collected by Fulcanelli in "Las Moradas Filosofales", which shows how SULPHUR is obtained from the first materias. Danae is the mineral of the mine, Perseus is the son of ZEUS and Danae (mineral and hermetic solvent).

DAMASCUS: From Damar, woman, alchemical Mercury.

DEE, John: Famous British occultist of the 16th century, author of the "Hieroglyphic Monad", 1613, now translated into Spanish.

DERNIER DU PAUVRE O LA PERFECTION DES METAUX: Book of 1785, published in Paris, much sought after by lovers of Alchemy.

DECOCCION: From the Latin decoquere, to cook, sometimes understood as to resolve, liquidify or reincrude.

DOLPHIN: Wren, little prince, also called Echneis or Remora, indicates at first WATER, cold and humid, the "mercury" of our work, which little by little coagulates by the action of SUGAR, which is the desiccating and fixing agent.

DESPERATION: The feeling of the blowers who ruined themselves in their laborious searches, wasting their money without getting results. It also indicates a lack of faith in the chemical and therapeutic procedures of Alchemy and Spagyrics, for the elaboration of remedies against illnesses.

It has led to the ruin of the works of impatient alchemists.

DISTILLATION: In Spagyric distillation coincides with that explained by modern chemists, cooling the vapours of the liquid in a coil.

The distillation of products is a usual operation of the alchemists.

For the antimonists, like Canseliet, it means something else, for them it is an alchemical operation that consists of the double moistening of the sulphur prior to the brief decoction of the "sublimations", from the Greek di, twice, and estilé, in small quantity.

DIANA: White Mercury. She is the goddess of hunting, also called ARTEMIS. Philaletheus outlined the great enigma of the Doves of Diana to explain the SUBLIMATIONS.

DIGESTION: Cooking at a low temperature, without causing the liquid to boil. It can be read in Lemery's book "Course de Chymie".

DIGBY: False alchemist of the 17th century, author of numerous swindles which made him famous. He carried out numerous public transmutations that served as propaganda for alchemy, with stone apparently obtained by illicit means.

DILUVIUM: Effect produced in the ALUDEL by the effect of the external fire, which excites the internal fire of the compound, which becomes liquid, agitated and swollen, with the sad appearance of a flood produced by the Universal Diluvium.

DISSOLUTION: Alchemical operation by means of which a third body is obtained from two bodies.

In the "Hermetic Triumph" of Limojon de St. Didier, it is said: "The solution of the body in its own blood is the solution of the male by means of the female, and that of the body by means of its spirit; it will be in vain for you to attempt to make the perfect solution of the body if you do not reiterate on the influx of its own blood, which is the whole of the natural "menstruation" of its "woman" and of its spirit, with which they are so closely united that they make but one substance".

Pedro Elías, in his unpublished "Opúsculo Pétreo", states that "the blood is a living water that irrigates the earth to make it germinate, changes the bodies into spirits, stripping them of their coarse earthiness, the mercury, when bathed by the spirit, dyes it and gives it the reddish colour of menstruation".

The main secret of Alchemy is precisely that of Dissolution, and it is necessary to cut out many of these operations, all similar in technique, though with different purposes. All the operations of Alchemy require a prior DISSOLUTION (digestion, putrefaction, maturation, circulation, etc.) and are the effects of the same cause.

UNIVERSAL SOLVENT: See Alkaest. This solvent dissolves only all the compounds involved in the Alchemical Magistery, so that the "research" of the blowers does not seem logical; the solvent which they did not find should dissolve the vessel containing them, as well as all the products without exception, including themselves.

Alkaest is made from a mineral SUBJECT, dry and fibrous in appearance, and requires expert handlers who know how to use it and the TRICK that its practice requires.

The metal, which must be dissolved, will be dissolved only with the aid of the most appropriate "metallic" solvent, our "magnesia", the first matter of the Work, SATURN or metallic Adam.

DOUBLE: Copy of something. In Alchemy the Rebis or double Mercury is obtained from sublimations. See Androgynous.

DRAGANTIUM: Vitriol. Living gold of the alchemists.

DRAGON: Alchemical Mercury and also the matter with which the work begins. It is the initial form of Mercury, our elder, son of Saurno.

The Dragon manifests itself throughout the work, dyeing the walls of the VESSEL containing the REBIS with colours; it is poisonous to the Stone, and yet necessary for the life of the compound.

Antimony was called Dragon in medium spagyrics, as well as grey wolf, because of its property of eating all metals alloyed with this metal.

DUJOLS, Pierre: Writing under the pseudonym of Magofonte, he was a Parisian bookseller at the beginning of the century, a connoisseur and writer of works on Alchemy.

DULCEDO SATURNI: The Soul of Lead.

BOILING: The action of boiling a liquid violently, breaking bubbles on the surface by the action of fire.

ECHNEIS: First solid state that the embryonic stone takes on, when the "mercury" absorbs the Secret Fire.

EGREGOR: Grouping of Souls. Alchemists and Templars are subject to the same Egregor, which is of the SOLAR type.

AXIS OF ART: Technique of the Philosophical Dissolution, necessary to practice the SOLVE ET COAGULA throughout the great work.

ELEAZAR: Name of Abraham the Jew, a character in Flamel's book of Hieroglyphic Figures.

ELEMENTS: Nature is composed of four elements, namely air, earth, water and fire, according to European Spagyrics, which, mixed in different proportions, determine the nature of any body. The metallic thesis of Spanish and later European Spagyrics considers the main components of metals to be elemental sulphur and mercury, whose composition is of the four elements.

In Alchemy, the definition of element is broader, as all the components and utensils involved in the elaboration process are considered as such, including the furnace or atanor, the apparatus and tools, the charcoal or gas for the fire, the compounds, the catalysts and the minerals used in the Great Work.

ELIXATION: The final phase of the Solar Regime, in which the ELIXIR or Universal Medicine, the all-healing Panacea, is obtained.

ELIXIR: Universal Medicine of Alchemy. It is the stone obtained at the end of the wet way, not yet oriented by gold for the medicine of metals. When this elixir has a great power, being of more than three "rotations" which have multiplied it in quality and quantity, it should be taken in an amount of 4 to 6 drops, as it is dangerous to ingest larger quantities.

ELECTRUM: A mixture of the seven planetary metals, brought together by fusion of the exact moments of the planetary conjunctions, as Paracelsus explains in the Archidoxia Magica, starting the alloy with the most volatile, which are mercury and lead, then tin, then silver, copper, iron and gold. The order of the last four is less important, but iron should be left for last. The applications of this metal are in sacred objects and in ancient jewellery to reinforce the astrological properties of the stones.

ELLIADE MIRCEA: Author of "Blacksmiths and Alchemists", a very curious essay, published by Editorial Nacional, which went bankrupt in 1987.

EMBLEM: Representation of something by a characteristic that defines it, in the style of hieroglyphics.

EMBLEMATIC: Relating to the emblem. Enigmatic, hieroglyphic representing one of the parts of the Great Work.

EMBRYON: Foetus, offspring in its mother's womb. In Alchemy it is used to designate the mercury that is born from CHAOS, because of its youth, then this mercurial child develops and becomes an adolescent. This word comes from the Greek Embryon.

OAK: Tree of the genus Quercus, like the oak, which by kabalistic-phonetic comparison is close to Hermes or Hermes, emblematic symbols of the alchemical Mercury. The holm oak is consecrated to Mars, in the distant Colchis.

The holm oak is the hieroglyph for the 1st matter of alchemy.

ENTRANCE: When a compound has the power to penetrate the matter it attacks. It is equivalent to "mordant" in modern chemistry. In alchemy, the power of penetration is required of the Philosopher's Stone, so that it "tinges" all metal subjected to its action in order to turn it into gold. This "incoming" power is one of the indices of quality, as well as the transmuting power expressed as the ratio of weights between the trans-mutated metal and the stone.

ENVY: Authors who tell only half-truths, in order that the knowledge of Science may not be vulgarised, are called envious; they are generally afraid that this wisdom may fall into the wrong hands, with consequent harm to society. That is why they That is why they never reveal their secret without the express permission of the Divinity.

EROS: Son of Zeus and Aphrodite, he is the common Mercury of the Alchemists.

EPISTOLA IGNE PHILOSOPHARUM: Manuscript of the Biblioteque National de Paris with the number 19.169.

SCALA PHILOSOPHARUM: Ten-step ladder representing the Great Work in its entirety, it is drawn on the first page of the Mutus Liber, as well as in the Cathedral of Notre Dame in Paris, it links the earth and the sky, as explained in "Betilo". The alchemist receives his inspiration by dreaming.

SCRUPLE: Unit of weight. 24 grams.

ALCHEMIST SCHOOLS:

* Chemical Alchemists:

- Antimonists: Those who work with antimony from stibnite and iron. Eugène Canseliet is worth mentioning.

- Galenists: Those who work with lead from galena and iron. Cleopatra is a case in point.

- Traditional: The character of the substances with which they operate is not indicated, because they are sensitive (like photographic films to light), to the psychic states of the operator, and such substances (two minerals) require the continuous attention and care of the alchemist, both to free the Azoth, and to obtain the Stone, that is why it is said that the alchemist himself is part of the formula, since he intervenes in the process. Examples include Philaletheus, Fulcanelli, Simon H., etc.

- Mental Alchemists:

- Alchemists of the mind: They consider man as an athanor in which the inner processes of self-transmutation take place; they seek spiritual development by the interpretation and practice of alchemical texts, in their own way, in the individual. The Barcelona school is worth mentioning.

- Sexual alchemists: They make an orgasmic interpretation of alchemy, through orgasm they transmute themselves into eternal beings, in the likeness of God.

ESSENCE: Pure, concentrated substance. Quintessence.

EMERALD: In Alchemy, the symbol of the Emerald, green in colour, is widely used, and has led to an article in the Revista Química e Industria with that name (section El Alquimista). In the first operation, when the grey wolf devours the Golden Ass, it turns green, becoming the "secret fire".

SWORD: It is the common mercury, capable of killing and resurrecting, mortifying and regenerating, destroying and organising.

SPAGYRIC: A science parallel to alchemy from which modern chemistry is derived, due to the erroneous interpretation of past alchemical texts. Paracelsus points it out as the bearer of the knowledge of the means used by the pharmacists to elaborate medicines from vegetables by alchemical techniques. Spagyricists in general know the Great Work only by reference. He is the first to openly deride the blowers whom he calmly calls "soot-burners", openly despising them, and warning of the trickery they are capable of in order to empty the wallet of the most astute who would believe them. The dry way is considered a spagyric method, suitable only for obtaining transmuting stone. Spagyric can be on minerals and vegetables.

ESPAGNET, President Jean D': 17th century Bordeaux alchemist, author of the "Philosophie Naturelle Retablie en sa Purete", Paris 1651, of which there is a copy in the National Library of Madrid.

SPIRIT: It comes from the Greek, it means seed, seed, it designates sulphur, mercury, catalysts or an infinite number of products depending on the authors and the paragraph that is read.

ESPIRIT GOBINEAU DE MOTLUISSANT: 15th century alchemist, author of the "Very curious explanation of the enigmas and hieroglyphic figures of..." (Ford treatises of alchemy, Ford treatises of alchemy, in the "Enigmas and hieroglyphic figures of..."). (Ford treatises on alchemy, published by Visión Libros).

SPIRIT: Any volatile or gaseous matter, any gas or vapour. The alchemical MERCURY.

- Astral Spirit: One of the names given to the dew, as well as that of the spirit of the world. Air of the Stone and alchemical Mercury.

- Universal Spirit: Coincides with the astral spirit, dew father of the secret fire of the alchemists. Alchemical Mercury.

- Fetid spirit: The fetidness symbolically exposes the decomposition and blackness of rottenness, so it is clear that it designates the raven, hieroglyph of sulphur.

WHITE WIFE: animated Mercury.

MOON SPUR: Synonym of the secret fire.

STIBINE: Mineral of sulphide composition of antinomium. It is currently known as Antimonite, it is very abundant in Spain, it is extracted from the mines of Alburquerque in Extremadura (Spain). It is hardly used in Alchemy: the "way of Antimony" is defined as being very difficult to obtain in the "Triumphal Chariot of Antimony" used by the Chinese.

MORNING STAR: This is the perfect sign of the work, it appears and disappears after the combats in which Mercury intervenes, and is the mute witness of the transformations that the alchemical bodies undergo internally. Note that this star is double; the first appears after the purification by fire and salt, announcing the conception of the alchemical embryo, the second crowns the child before birth. It is the six-pointed star, the seal of Solomon, the sign of pacification and procreation, the signature of the Theme of the Wise.

EVA: Feminine principle, Adam's wife who in the Eagles sublimates and conforms to him little by little as she dissolves him in her womb, giving him properties of softness and fixity in the face of fire.

EVESTRUM: Philosopher's Stone about to be realised.

EVOLA, Julius: Contemporary Italian occultist, author of the "Hermetic Tradition", published by the Other Science Collection, and of several essays on the Holy Grail, published by Plaza & Janes.

EXALTATION: To increase the properties of an alchemical compound, in order to make it more suitable for the execution of the work of Hercules in alchemical manipulation.

EXECATION: a From the Latin Exicatio, to desire. It is produced as the humidity disappears after the beginning of each Regimen.

- F -

FACINUN: Copper.

FACTION: From the Latin factio, operation, action of doing, accomplishing or finishing. Another meaning is that of finishing complete parts of a work or of a chemical or alchemical operation.

FEBIGENO: It comes from the Greek words Feo, hieroglyphic solar god of gold, and genos, to generate. It is the "Son of gold" or the being engendered by it.

PHOENIX: Bird that lives in fire and rises from its own ashes, like the alchemical Mercury.

FERMENT: From the Latin fermentum, yeast that causes bread to swell. There is an allegory that equates the work of alchemy with that of baking. The ferment is the compound that causes the reaction within the materials that make up the Philosopher's Egg.

FERMENTATION: Catalytic action of the salts extracted from the dew in any of the phases of the Hermetic Work.

FIEL: Piece of the balance that indicates the rightness of the weight. Person who keeps a secret (from the Latin feal). Person who follows a method without deviating into error, step by step according to the technical and spiritual "norms" that the fulfilment of the Art demands.

FIX: Alchemist term that describes the action of a compound such as sulphur, which does not volatilise in fire, on mercury, which becomes more fusible and less volatile as the Great Work progresses.

FIGUIER, Louis: 19th century scientist and writer, lover of the Science of Hermes, author of "L' alchimie et les Alchimistes", Hachette, Paris 1856.

FILALETEO, IRINEO: Probable pseudonym of Tomas Vaugham, however in the National Library of Madrid, his works are registered under the name of George Starkey. An extraordinary alchemist, English by birth, he lived in the 17th century, and was seen in North America in the following century, his works are worth mentioning;

- The Open Entrance to the King's Palace (Introitus), Ed 71/2 and the Theophilus Edition. The French translation is by Lenglet du Fresnoi, Amsterdam 1667.

- "Brief Guide to the Celestial Ruby."

- "Obtaining the Mercury of the Philosophers from the Starry Martial Regulus."

"The Fountain of the Sapientia Chemica," 1669.

- "Speculum Veritatis", drawing book in the Vatican Library.

All his known works are available to the average reader in Spain.

PHILOSOPHER: A person who lives in seclusion and studies natural laws, as defined by the Dictionary of the Royal Spanish Academy of Language. The Hermetic philosopher studies Alchemy, he follows the steps of Nature step by step.

PHILOSOPHY: Another name for Alchemy, also called Natural Philosophy, because of the demands it makes on its followers.

FLAMEL, Nicolas: 14th century Parisian alchemist, who was buried at the beginning of the 15th century, and who is said to be still alive, the Abbot Villane kept many of the notes on Flamel's life. The best known books of the famous author are:

- "The Book of Hieroglyphic Figures", Ed. Obelisco, Barcelona.

- "Le Livre des laveures".

- "Le Sommaire Philosophique".

- "Le dessir dessirée".

FLANMARION, Camile: Astronomer, researcher and wise man from neighbouring France, died in 1925, wrote on esoteric subjects, researching on death; among other subjects he touches on Alchemy.

FLOWER: Aspects that the alchemical mercury takes on throughout life. The first flower is the black rose, from which the Mirror of Art is extracted.

FONS FILOSORUM: Bath of Mary.

FRAGUADOR: A person who makes his fortune by deceitful trickery, pretends to be a genuine alchemist, and makes his living and wealth on the backs of others, on the basis of supposedly hermetic knowledge.

The name of forger is also given to failed alchemists who undertook research along erroneous paths, generally through ignorance of what they were supposed to be looking for; these forgers suffered painful circumstances in their laborious searches that gave knowledge to chemistry, and which led to the physical and economic ruin of many of them.

He is also called a forger who only uses particulars for the transmutation of the metals, by the use of the FORGE of the spagyrists.

FREQUENCY: It comes from the Latin frequency, union in the same place of several. It also indicates the male-female sexual relationship. In the human simile of Alchemy, the manly sulphur frequents the mercurial lady, who welcomes his "favours" with the passion of mineral reactions, in the various stony regimes.

FRRIGIDITY: It comes from the Latin frigiditas, it is a quality inherent to the earth, opposed to elemental fire, it is a sign of cold, of lack of light and heat, of blackness, of putrefaction, death, of the "raven" or sulphur.

FIRE: It is one of the 4 elements, it is part of all matter and is energy. There is a correlation between the degrees of fire and sulphur, the four degrees of fire correspond to the four degrees of sulphur. Their representation is.

The alchemists consider many types of fire, of which it is worth mentioning:

- Unnatural fire: The one produced by the combustion of inflammable materials.

- Natural fire: The energy emitted by the sun, the moon, the stars, volcanoes, radioactivity, and all energy emitted by nature when it is not artificially forced to emit it.

- Secret or Sophic Fire: This is contained in the interior of matter, in the catalysts of Alchemy, it has the property that the vulgar fire excites it, and produces the slow turning of the wheel, which produces the phenomena observable inside the alchemical flask; it is contained in the GREEN mercury.

Philaletheus identifies it with the agent that makes the axle move and the wheel turn. Limojon explains that it is the only agent that makes the water that does not wet the hands of our first matter, the source of LIVING WATER, gush forth.

- Wheel fire: Cyclic rotation of the mercury in order to multiply the Stone, it consists of passing through all the regimes, including that of Mercury, after dissolving the Stone.

- Fire of ashes: Bath of sand.

- Source: This word has several meanings in general use, as Fulcanelli points out in the Mystery of the Cathedrals.

- Mysterious Fountain: The Pontic Water that is drawn from the Ore of the Wise in the 1st operation.

- Source of life: Universal Spirit that nourishes the earth in the springtime, with the infinitesimal contribution of the rare earths and salts that fecundate the world, provoking the multiplication of the species. Green Alchemical Mercury.

- Fountain of Youth: The legends of the search for the fountain of Ethereal Youth are everywhere on the Planet. This source is none other than Alchemy itself, which puts at the disposal of the Artist a good quantity of products capable of improving his health, prolonging his life to the limits that God has set.

FULCANELLI: A contemporary French alchemist who has managed to remain anonymous, to the extent that it is impossible to know his identity. The Americans sought him out for having defined the geometric characteristics of a nuclear reactor, according to Jacques Bergier, before any had been built.

The works are translated into Spanish and published by Plaza y Janes; they are:

- "The Mystery of the Cathedrals".

- Las Moradas Filosofales".

Death" surprised him without having finished the alchemical trilogy with the work "Finis Gloria Mundi", of which Canseliet had the original manuscript, and which he cites in his works, without having published it.

FUSIBLE: Fusible, which can be melted and reduced to liquor. Catalyst in a chemical reaction.

GALENA: Lead Sulphide Ore used by GALENISTS as a source of AZOTH.

GALENISTS: Alchemists who use galena as the raw material of the Work.

GALLO: Hieroglyph for Philosophical Mercury, which in itself is very volatile. The fable of the cock and the fox explains the procedure of the dry way.

GANZENMULLER, W Contemporary researcher, author of "L' Alchimie du moyen Age" Editions Aubier 1940.

GEBER: Arab philosopher of the 18th century to whom numerous works on alchemy are attributed, the most famous of which is the "Summa perfectionis".

GERBERT: Alchemist pope known as Sylvester II.

GERMINATIVE: The power of the alchemical catalysts to give "life" to Mercury, giving it the force and power to produce the turning of the Wheel.

GLAUBERT, Rudolf: 17th century German alchemist, witness of numerous transmutations, author of "Opera Chemica" 1658.

GRAAL: See Grail.

GREAT WORK: Compilation of the works of Hercu¬les, which develop the whole of Alchemy, including the operations, the products, the works and all that is involved in obtaining the precious Gift of God.

GRAIN: A unit of weight of 0.053 grams.

GRAIL: The medieval hieroglyph for the alchemical Mercury, for immaterial objects, for the Stone of the Wise, for the Chemical Light and for the vessel of Hermes. It is the sacred deposit that contained the Blood of Christ.

Christiën de Troyes makes the following cabalistic lucubration of the evolution of the word: Holy Grail --> Blood --> Royal Blood --> Royal Blood: It is the product that Flamel points out as the Blood of the Innocents and Raymond as the Menstruum emanated from the mercurial "lady".

The virtues of the Grail are:

- Power to give supernatural illuminating force.

- Nourishing power for the Stone.

- By virtue of the Grail the Phoenix is consumed and turns to ash, the mercury is transformed and becomes more beautiful.

- It is both a life-giving and a destructive force.

- It is the inciter of the forces of domination and victory.

All virtues must be understood in their strictest alchemical sense.

GRIFFLE: Mythological animal, used by alchemists as a hieroglyph for the preparation of the raw materials of the Work, showing the result of the operation after the chemical meeting of the materials.

GRILLOT DE GIVRY: Contemporary occultist, author of famous texts that are hardly related to alchemy, although their lexicon coincides:

- "The Great Work", Ed. 7 1/2.

- "The Museum of Witches, Magicians and Alchemists", Ed.Tchou, Paris, 1866.

GREY: The emblematic colour of Fire in antiquity. The names of highly flammable products are given names with the root "grey", e.g., the grey gas from coal mines and swamps, equivalent to "fire fatuous", "fire gas". Some further references can be read in Cristóbal (san).

GROS: Unit of weight of 3.82 grams. Equivalent to 72 "grains".

GRUESA: Twelve dozen. Unit of weight.

H, Simon: Contemporary alchemist from Madrid, author of numerous works on alchemy, among which we should mention:

- "La Puerta Cerrada, diario de un alquimista" (The Closed Door, diary of an alchemist).

- "Las Palomas de Diana y La Medicina Universal" (Diana's Doves and University Medicine).

- "The Golden Book of Alchemy".

- "Alchemy, the Enigma of the Ages".

- "Alchemy, the Seven Times".

As an alchemist he is well known, and has founded the school of modern alchemists, which in my opinion is the most important in the world, following the traditional line, spreading his movements from Spain to the whole world, just as the School of Translators of Toledo did centuries before.

HÄMILTON, Jones J.W.: Contemporary author of "Bacstrom's Chemical Anthology", 1960.

HAL: Salt.

FAECES: Word from the Latin Foeces, with the meaning of waste, rubbish, slime, dung, excrement, filth, dirt, filth, dregs, sediment, and impurity. In decantations it is the dregs that go to the bottom of the vessel. In eagles it is the residue known as the dead earth of the Stone.

HEL: Honey.

HELVETIUS, John Frederick: 17th century Dutch physician, author of Vitulus "Aureus", Amsterdam 1667.

HERMAPHRODITE: See Androgynous, a word of which it is a synonym, composed of two Greek words, Hermes, the mercurial hieroglyph, the feminine principle of the Work, and Aphrodite, Goddess of Love, the anagram of Venus, the hieroglyph of the Sulphur, the masculine principle in the phylosophical elaboration. The Hermaphrodite is thus a compound of Sulphur and Mercury, possessing the qualities of male and female, of man and woman, and is one of the names of the Mercury treated by the sublimations which prepare it for the realisation of the Work in the form of AZOTH. The Hermaphrodite is therefore synonymous with the Philosophical Mercury.

HERMES TRIMEGISTUS: Words from the Greek, indicating Hermes three times great.

Hermes was worshipped by the Greeks as God, they attributed to him the foundation of the Alchemical Science and the paternity of several hundreds of treatises on the subject; nowadays it is on the market translated into Spanish:

- "Three Esoteric Treatises" (Poimandrés, Asclepios and one other).

- The Golden Treatise 1692.

- "The Emerald Tablet".

- "Twelve Chapters of Hermes".

"The Labours of Hercules", Luis Cárcamo Ed.

- "The Testament".

- "The Secret of the Physical Stone".

Hermes in Alchemy is synonymous with "Mercury", since the whole Work is carried out with Alchemical Mercury.

HERMETIC: Referring to Hermes Trismegistus or his teachings. Referring to Alchemy or Occultism.

A perfectly polished vessel, sealed in such a way as to make it impossible, even when there is pressure in it, for a gas to escape or penetrate.

Body endowed with the Seal of Hermes, a six-pointed Solomonic star, characteristic of Alchemical Mercury.

HETEROGENEOUS: Not homogeneous, varied, with parts of various and diverse natures, with diversity without uniformity.

HEVILATH: Living earth from which the "magic" gold is born, of extraordinary heat and dryness, it was used for the designation of the natural mineral, as it is obtained in its crude state. It is the raw alchemical "sulphur", before extraction.

IRON: Metal of great importance for spagyrics, the SULPHUR of iron (Mars) is the most active, according to Fulcanelli, and the closest to GOLD.

SON OF SATURN: The product of the 1st operation according to the author of the Medulla of Alchemy.

FIGUERA: According to Fulcanelli, it is the Virgin Mother carrying her child.

ARIANA'S THREAD: Indications that enable the student to unravel the mysteries of Alchemy, to follow it step by step; it is the hieroglyphic of the Labyrinth of the Minotaur and the indication of not having gone astray in the paths of the Great Work.

In order not to go astray in the preparations of matter, it is advisable to leave reference points along the way, throughout the operations.

HOLMYARD, E.J.: German author who has translated Geber, researcher of the alchemical theme, the following works can be mentioned to his credit:

"History of Alchemy", Guadiana Ed.

- Alchemy", Artaud Ed.

DOUBLE MAN, igneous mountain: Expression of Basil Valentine, expressing the duplicity of the Animated Mercury. Other authors maintain that it is a name of the Sal Harmoniaco.

RED MAN: Hieroglyph of the 3rd matter of Alchemy. It is also a hieroglyph for "ADAM".

HORIZONTIS: Elixir of long life.

PHILOSOPHICAL OVEN: Atanor.

HORTULAN: Ancient alchemist who commented on the obscure Emerald Tablet even more obscurely, which made him famous. He is considered a "classic" by today's alchemists.

HORUS: Egyptian god born of Isis, the Moon and Osiris (the Sun). He is the hieroglyph for Solar Sulphur. The Tabula Smeragdina of Hermes says: Pater eius sol, mater eius Moon (his father is the Sun, his mother is the Moon).

PHILOSOPHICAL EGG: It is the vessel that contains the philosophical matter. Most of the time when referring to the egg, one must include the products it contains in its inner secret, which are those of the dry and wet ways.

In analogy to the Animal Kingdom, the egg is incubated in the athanor, until the matter it contains consumes the reaction. The vessel is removed at the end of each Regimen.

ADAMIC BONE: A yellowish product resembling crushed bone, which is none other than the Alchemical Adam, according to the thesis of the antimonists.

HUGGINS DE BARNA: Alchemist of the Via Seca, author of "The Regime of Saturn changed into the Golden Age".

RADICAL WATER: One of the matters of the Sages, which has the character of "water", i.e. liquid. Sometimes it is Mercury, sometimes it is the Universal Spirit. With this confidence the secret of Flamel "Wash with fire, burn with water" is understood.

HUSSON BERNARD: Contemporary Gallic author, compiled "Two Hermetic Treatises of the 19th century" (Hermes Unveiled, Cambriel's Course of Hermetic Philosophy), Omnium Litteraire, 1964.

HUTTIN, Serge: Modern writer author of:

- "L'Alchimie", Collection "Que j'ais sais"?

-Les Alchimistes", Editions du Sevrill, Paris 1964.

HYLE: Primordial matter of the Philosopher's Stone.

IGNEUS: It comes from the Latin Igneus, indicating that its nature is of fire. This appellation is typical of IMAN, SULPHUR, Philosophical Mercury, and above all of the finished Philosopher's Stone itself.

IGNIS LEONIS: Secret alchemical fire.

IMBIBITION: Technique to apply the SOLVENT, irrigating little by little the body in digestion.

FIREPROOF: The property of sulphur of not burning in the fire, it is a synonym of fixity, of incolumne permanence in the flame.

INDISSOLUBLE: Property of double mercury, which cannot be separated into the original mercury and sulphur without destroying them; it is a perfect alchemical marriage.

INFLUENCES: Verifiable physical effects on chemical reactions, caused by the passage of a star, the phase of the moon, the time of the year, solar or lunar radiation, the season of the year, etc.

-   Effects of a catalyst on a reaction.

-   Poisoning of a chemical reaction.

BURNER: Burner, fuelled by coal, alcohol, gas, electricity, etc., used as an auxiliary in alchemical operations, but not involved in the direct execution of the work. An example is the Bunsen burner.

HELL: Lower part of the atanor in which the combustion of the coal takes place, lower part of the vessel in which the "sulphur" or MOSZACUMIA is deposited. A hot area due to geothermal action and a place in Israel, feared for being a terrible tremble.

INGENUITI: From the Latin Ingenium, machine, instrument. Philaletheus uses it in the sense of spiritual and mental acuity, which is required to understand his writings.

INSOLUBLE: In Spagyria it is applied to bodies that do not dissolve in others. It is also used to indicate the unaffordability of a subject because it is very complicated, so that Alchemy is considered an enigma by the neophyte.

MAGNET: Alchemical hieroglyph for the Second Raw Material of the Great Work.

The steel attracts the MAGNET to it, just as the MAGNET turns to the Steel, says Philaletheus.

ISIS: Egyptian Goddess, whose statuettes are always black, passed on to Christianity while retaining her image of Virgin and Mother given by the traditional Religion of the Mysteries, she is the hieroglyphic of our Chaos, a black, heavy, brittle substance, extracted from the mother mineral of Alchemy (or mine): Isis is the Moon Goddess, hieroglyphic of our Mercury.

PHILOSOPHIC ISLAND: Island of Delos. The first coagulation of the rising SULPHUR.

JAKIM: One of the columns of the Temple of Solomon.

JIHAD: Holy war of Islamics, between Mercury and Sulphur, which battle after battle reiterates the combat, resulting in the AZOTH.

JOLIVET - CASTELOT: Spagyric of the beginning of the century.

JOHN XXII: Alchemist Pope, tireless persecutor of the other alchemists against whom he published a Bull. He manufactured a considerable quantity of gold during his mandate, which was very brief. He wrote a treaty of Alchemy: "Ars Transmutatoria", Lyon 1557.

JUNO: A name from JUPITER.

JUPITER: Spagyric name of Tin, and of its governing plant. Name of a Regime of the Great Work, the next to that of Saturn.

- K -

KA: An Egyptian idiom, meaning soul, hardly used in its mineral sense since the 3rd century AD. It is the hieroglyph for the alchemical SULPHUR.

KADUSH: The Sun.

KALNOS: Iron, not "copper".

KAMALA-JNANA: Author of the "Dictionaire de Philosophie Alchimiste", Ed. Charlet 1961.

KELLY, Eduard: Lived in England in the 16th century, swindled in the shadow of John Dee's prestige, and became very famous. He is the author of the "Book of St. Dunstans" Alchemical Writings 1893.

KERMES: Tree of the genus Quercus, the holm oak, hieroglyphic of the first matter and anagram of Hermes Trismegistus, elder and Mercury. Another antimony mineral is also called Kermesite. See OAK.

KERVRAN, Louis C: Current researcher, author of "Transmutations Biologiques", Librairie Maloine, 1963.

KUNRATH, Heinrich: 17th century alchemist, author of "Anphiteatrum Sapientiae Eternae" 1609.

KUPRIS: The Impure, Venus, Copper.

- L -

LABYRINTH: Solomon's labyrinths are concentric circles, interrupted at points that show us an inextricable path, to get out of which we need Ariadne's thread. In the labyrinth was the battle of Theseus and the Minotaur, symbols of the two natures of sulphur and mercury.

The labyrinth is the hieroglyph of the whole Great Work.

LABOR: From the Latin labor, work. The improbus labor are the Labours of Hercules, which the alchemist needs to perform for the culmination of the Work, and which correspond to the Regime of Mercury or the preparation of substances.

LAMINAS: From the Latin Laminas, little leaves, they characterise the animated Mercury which takes on the appearance of a leaf, its hieroglyph being the open book.

LAPILS: See Lapis.

LAPIS: Stone, used to indicate the Philosopher's Stone in numerous meanings; Lapis ignis, lapis philosopharum, etc.

LAPIDARY: A person knowledgeable in stones, a cutter and scholar of them, nowadays they are called gemologists, or geologists, depending on the speciality.

Text that deals with stones, such as that of Alfonso X the Wise King (Spain).

LASCARIS: 18th century alchemist, famous for his public transmutations.

LATOM: Philosophical Mercury before the blackness.

LATON (Brass): Equivalent to LATONA, Copper, Bronze, Venus and CIPRINA, hieroglyphs of the 2nd Matter of the Great Work.

LATONA (Leto): Mother of Apollo (the Sun) and Artemis (Diana, the Moon), children of ZEUS.

The face of Latona must be washed with her "blood", that is to say, with the WATER extracted from her, by dissolution.

LATRO: The Mercury.

LAVOISIER, Antoine Laurent: French chemist of the 18th century, author of the Chemical Law of his name, very interested in the themes of Alchemy, a science which had not yet fallen into the disrepute of the 19th and part of the 20th century, in which it resurfaced with great force.

LAURENTINO: See Laurentian Fields.

LOYAL SERVANT: The Alchemical Mercury, who serves the alchemist throughout the whole Work.

MILK OF THE VIRGIN: Another name for Mercury, a liquor extracted from Magnesia, and which springs from the CHAOS of the Wise.

LEIBNITZ, Gottfried Wilhein: Philosopher and mathematician of the 17th century, died in 1716.

LENGLET DU FRESNOI, Nicolas: Priest and historian of the 17th century, alchemist, died at the foot of the atanor, falling asleep over the fire he was watching at the age of eighty. He is the author of "L'Historie de la Philosophie hermètique", Amsterdam 1742.

BRASS (LATON): Hieroglyph of sulphur, it represents the King of the terrestrial animals, it is the symbol of Alchemical Gold and metallic Gold, sometimes it is the Sophic Fire or the receptive matter of the Universal Spirit.

> Green Lion: Anagram of the Metallic Youth, Chicken of Hermes, Food of Hyperion. In Alchemy it is the Hieroglyph of the 2nd Mastery of the Work, the receptive matter of the Secret Fire in the elaboration of the Dissolvent.

> Red Lion: Another name for the Gold of the Philosophers, this is also the name given to the "monster" known to Flamel as the Sanctuary of the Innocents, which is obtained from the Green Brass.

It is also the hieroglyph of the 3rd Matéria of the Great Work, which dispenses SALT.

Brass and Lioness: Pair of compounds which, united, give rise to the "Mirror of Art".

LIAB: Vinegar.

LIBETHRA: Mercury comes from a SOURCE whose origin is MAGNESIA and the MAGNET. The source is called LIBETHRA.

LIBRA: Sign of the Zodiac from September 22nd to October 21st. In Alchemy it is used as a hieroglyph for the dosages that must be in accordance with the proportionate weight (Law of chemical proportions, or of Justice in weight).

BOOK: Emblem of Mercury

Closed book: Hieroglyph of the mercurial matter.

Open book: Hieroglyph of the prepared "mercury".

BOOK OF SET: Book of Alchemy from the 6th century.

LICOR AQUILEGIUS: Distilled wine.

HARE: Hieroglyph of the Mercury pointed out by Fulcanelli.

LIGACY: Tailing, the whipping of the glass, hermetic sealing. The result of completing a chemical reaction, by which the products are combined, hermetically sealed in a new substance.

LINEAR: From the Latin line, applied to the manner of carrying the athanor, the regime of fire grows gradually, little by little, as the Work progresses. This arcanum is closely guarded by the alchemists, who speak of the SEASONS.

LIMOJON DE ST.DIDIER: One of the French alchemists, whose texts are now appreciated by the whole world. This 17th century author wrote the following treatises:

- "The Ancient War of the Knights, or Discourse of the Philosopher's Stone and Gold", published by Plaza y Janés.

- The Hermetic Triumph", also published by the same publisher in the same text.

LIQUEFACTION: Operation by which a solid is reduced to a liquid. Fusion. Melting

WOLF: Hieroglyph for the alchemical Mercury. Spagyricists call ANTIMONY.

- Green wolf: Mercury in the 1st operation.

- Grey wolf: Mercury in the beginning.

CRAZY OF THE GREAT WORK: The alchemical Mercury.

LULIO, Raimundo: Majorcan alchemist of the 13th century, he became famous for his very curious and bizarre works on religious and philosophical themes. Numerous works of alchemy are attributed to him, which he was unable to write due to lack of time, among which the following stand out:

- "The Testament".

- The Codicil.

- The Clavicle".

- De Alchimia, Magia Naturali", etc.

Numerous editions of his books are published in the National Library in Madrid, almost all of them in Latin, but almost all of them have been translated into Castilian and Catalan.

LUCIFER: The bearer of the Light, of the Star, the Alchemical Mercury.

MOON: Planet astrologically attuned to Silver, the metal it symbolically represents. Alchemical mercury is a lunar metal called "living silver" by the ancient authors, and responds greatly to the influences of this star. Another metal is also of lunar influence, the Ancient Lesser Moon of the Spagyrics, arsenic, which has caused much displeasure among them.

In the wet way, the Regime of the Moon is considered the phase of the Great Work, although the white astral stone is obtained.

- Hermetic Moon: Living water, philosophical mercury.

LUNAR (MOON), Juice of the: Term used by Irineus Philaleteus to designate the alchemical Mercury.

LUT: The mortar made by philosophers to harden or grease their crystal glasses, in order to make them more resistant to fire.

TO LUT: Word coming from the Latin Lutum, tallow. This operation consists of sealing all the openings of a vessel with tallow so that it does not breathe. The hermetically sealed vessel prevents the transfer of vapours and volatile products into the atmosphere, which is of paramount importance in practical alchemy.

KEYS: Name given by the alchemists to all irreducible radical "dissolution" and to the monsters that cause them (chemical reactions).

Name of a complete regime or of a complete part of an operation of a Regime of the Great Work.

The keys to SUCCESS in the Great Work are manifested by DARKNESS; if it is present you are almost certainly on the right track, as the TREVISAN has said.

CRIE: "Cry" of the metal when it is being worked.

MACERATION: Operation of Vegetal Spagyrics by which the plants to be extracted are subjected to the action of water, wine or vinegar, previously crushed, and for a few days, hours or years, depending on the nature of the plant.

MOTHER: First matter of the Great Work.

MATURATION: Time necessary to complete each of the Regimes of the Work, and which cannot be shortened by the alchemist.

MAGISTERY: Comes from the Latin Magisterium, teaching. It comprises the detailed theoretical and practical knowledge of all the steps and elements involved in Alchemy.

Magisteriums are the spagyric teachings for the preparation of metals and alloys, which trained the smelters of the time. The name is still used today for teacher training colleges.

Alchemical Magistery: Knowledge and practice of the Philosopher's Stone.

MAGNESIA: Term of Art used by Irineo Filaleteo to indicate the Alchemical Mercury. In Spagyrics, as well as magnesium, it was used to refer to talc and the Magnet Stone, it is also used to designate some metallic alloys, and the very magnesia (MgO) of chemists.

In Alchemy, "magnesia" indicates crude matter that attracts the "Magnet" and is hidden under the hard crust of the "steel" of the sages.

MAGOFONTE: Pseudonym of the French bookseller Pierre Dujols.

MAIER, Michel: Doctor and alchemist of the 17th century, author and draughtsman of the "Atlanta Fulgiens" 1618, reproduced by the Librerie de Médicis in 1969 with notes by Etiènne Perrot.

MANGUET, Jean Jacques: Geneva physician and 17th century alchemist, author of "La Bibliothèque Chimique Curieuse".

SEA: The sea in alchemy is identified with the Mercury, in which the unique and mysterious fish called Echneis, Remora or Dolphin (Little Prince) is fished.

MARCAR, René: Contemporary author of the "Petite Historie de la Chimie et de la Alchimie", Ed. Delmás Burdeaux, 1938.

MARTIAN: Of iron.

MARY THE JEW: Woman to whom is attributed the invention of the Bath Mary, she is the author of the "Dialogue of Mary and Aros on the Magisterium of Hermes", Salmon Vol 1. She is supposed to have lived in Alexandria in the 4th century AD.

MARS: Symbol and planet of iron. One of the regimes of the Work is so called, and is the one which precedes the Regime of the Sun in the third work.

MATERIAL: Any product or "theme" of those involved in the making of the Stone of the Wise.

These materials are three, they will produce SALT, MERCURY and SULPHUR, that is, the BODY, the SPIRIT and the SOUL, respectively. All three matters are necessary for life, and without them it cannot exist.

MATRIX: A bottle-like apparatus, made of glass, used by chemists and alchemists in their reactions.

Name of any temple dedicated to the Mother, e.g. Nôtre Dâme in Paris. The alchemists continually remind us of the cabalistic relationship between Mater (mother) and Materea (matter), which unites the Virgin with the First Matter.

Flask with the compound, prepared for and during the reaction.

MEDIATOR: The alchemical mercury, which appears embodied in the form of black salt, and hides within itself the "magic steel", marked by the star of its rays.

UNIVERSAL MEDICINE: Name given to the stone obtained by the wet way. All-healing panacea (medicinally, not surgically), with an oily appearance, characteristic odour and taste.

ORE OF THE WISE: Chaos or basic mineral of Alchemy.

MENSTRUUM: Liquid compound of RED colour. The "Blood of the Innocents" of Flamel.

MERCURY: In Spagyrics it is the liquid metal called quicksilver by the Branch of Glass. In Alchemy it is the alchemical Mercury, also known as the "Mirror of Art". Philalete teaches that it is a "child" which they form not by creating it, but by extracting it from the things in which it is enclosed, with the co-operation of Nature, and by a marvellous Artifice, so that it is not on Earth prepared and ready for the Work.

The alchemists consider it the SWORD of the artist.

- Black Mercury: First Mercury, extracted from the mineral MENA.

- White Mercury: Azoth.

- Philosophical Mercury: Azoth.

- Common Mercury: Universal Solvent.

- Red Mercury: Vinegar of the Philosophers, very sour.

- Animated Mercury: Azoth.

- Double Mercury: Azoth.

The Mercury Regime is the first of the Work and the most complicated, which is completed by the execution of the sublimations and the obtaining of the AZOTH.

METALS: Metallic bodies, those known to Chemistry.

- Dead metals: Metals that have been melted during their production, or throughout their life, remaining immobilised in their metallic "evolution".

- Reincrusted metals: Metals subjected to the action of Alkaest, recovering their condition of young and alive metals.

- Living metals: Metals in their mineral matrix.

MINE: See ORE.

MINERVA: The Goddess of War. See DIANA.

MYSTERY: Arcane, secret, hidden, very hidden.

MONDIFICATION: To peel, to remove dirt. In Alchemy it is done on the Eagles because they cleanse Mercury, leaving it immaculate white.

MORHOFF, George: 17th century medical alchemist.

MORIEN: Roman alchemist resident in Alexandria, lived in the 10th and 11th century, author of the "Conversations with King Calid and the Philosopher Morienus".

MOSZHACUMIA: Name of the faeces, filth of the "Vessel", such as the "Dead Earth of the Stone", and the draconic "husk" adhering to the vessel.

MULTIPLICATE: Rotation of the Alchemical Wheel, which serves to obtain a Stone of tenfold power in comparison with the previous one, as well as a greater quantity of Stone. The multiplication is in quantity and quality at the same time, and consists in dissolving one weight of Stony Sulphur in 10 times its weight of dissolving Mercury, after reiterating the Regimens.

TO MUTE: Synonymous with transmute. In any case, it indicates great modifications of the internal structure of a body, and even in spagyrics they are indicated by the STAR of David, or 6-pointed star.

NATURE: The alchemist expression "to follow Nature" implies the orderly following of the precise steps, in order to achieve a correct development of the successive alchemical operations, to obtain the Ph. Stone.

The study of the three Kingdoms of Nature is considered by alchemists as equal, because for them the three kingdoms are alive, and undergo a generally positive evolution for all their creatures. The best known part of alchemical studies is the Theory of Mineral Evolution, by which Mother Nature produces by "digestion" the evolution of metals and minerals, which are born, grow, develop and die, but not before they have reproduced themselves, even if only slowly and in the interior of the earth. This theory remains intact in the present time, among the few existing alchemists, in spite of the fact that it is repudiated and criticised by modern chemistry.

HERMETIC VESSEL: alchemical sulphur. See DELOS.

NEST or SAND: Part of the ATANOR in which the philosophical vessel rests.

NITRO: Salt of the Stone, obtained from the terrestrial matter, is fixed with a passive alkaline principle, which makes it material. In Spagyrics it is potassium nitrate.

NOSTOC: Microscopic algae that appears in the fields, evaporating as soon as the sun rises. It is used comparatively with the primordial Dew, highly volatile, it confused many researchers in the past, who did not know how to recognise in the expression the Spiritus Mundii, which is extracted from the Ore of sages.

GOLDEN KNOT: Allegory used by Fulcanelli to explain the obtaining of the alchemical SUGAR.

ALCHEMICAL NUPTIES: Alchemical wedding to obtain the AZOTH. Topic that has originated the writing of the "Chemical Wedding" by Cristian Rosenkreutz.

OBJECT OF ART: Alchemical term for the "chaotic" subject with which the Mirror of Art is elaborated.

WORK: From the Latin opera, opera, operation, completely encompassing the alchemical Magisterium.

> - Work of Saturn: Dry path of alchemy. Method which enables the transmutatory stone (or Sulphur) to be obtained in a short period of eight days, but which does not serve to attain the Universal Medicine.

> - Great Work: A wet method, of great length of time, which enables one to attain the Universal Medicine.

> - Minor Work: Mineral and vegetable spagyrics.

SMELLS: The stone has a special smell in each Regimen.

EAST: The point at which the sun rises and the light rises from the darkness. The star of the Work will evolve circularly, passing from black to citrine white and then to ruby, through the different Regimes.

There is a Masonic logic by the name of the "Spanish Grand Orient", with its headquarters in the Capital of Spain.

GOLD: King metal whose ruling planet is the Sun. It is represented by a circle with a zenithal point. It is the most perfect metal, of higher density than commercial mercury, in which it does not float, stainless and unassailable by most acids, it dissolves in the Harmoniac Salt, and is a symbol of perfection. The stone is the fruit of the Sun Tree.

- Alchemical Gold: Metal produced by the transmutation of another metal into gold, either by a spagyric particular or by the effect of the Transmuting Stone. Alchemical SULPHUR is usually referred to as such.

- Astral Gold: Energy emitted by the Sun, the Moon or another Planet, which is captured by the Mercury at the beginning of the work, and facilitates the crystallisation of the Alchemical Sulphur.

- White Gold: The name of the White Stone, suitable for the transmutation of metals into silver, obtained in the Moon Regime.

- Common Gold: Noble yellow metal used by jewellers. Alchemical sulphur.

- Gold of the Philosophers: Alchemical sulphur; its composition is neither sulphur nor gold.

- Red Gold: Adamic male. Wingless dragon. Blood of the Stone. Finished Philosopher's Stone.

- Potable Gold: It is the Universal Panacea, used to achieve Animal or Human health effects.

This word is attributed to Paracelsus, and has nothing to do with the dissolution of gold which is supposed to have been manufactured by the spagyrists of the time, as a medicine for all ills.

- Philosophical Gold: Of a colour like ashes, it is the internal fire and masculine agent of the Work, very volatile, its matter applied to the fire burns in the air without leaving a scintillating residue. The Philosophical Gold, once separated and FUSED, becomes total, natural and very pure GOLD, but it loses its value for Alchemy. If the melting temperature is not reached, it becomes the ASH called Philosophical Gold.

ORINAL: From the Latin Urna. It is a glass flask used as a vessel by alchemists and spagyrists, in which they kept the "urine salt".

OROPIMENT: Arsenic sulphide in its mineral form, which has been systematically used by philosophers to conceal the primary chaotic Subject of the Great Work. This metal has caused many poisonings, but it is less toxic than quicksilver. It was used to poison Napoleon on the Island of St. Helena.

OSIRIS: Solar god of the Egyptians, hieroglyph of Sulphur.

OUROBOROS: Hermes defines them as follows: "Serpens cuius caudam devorabit", snake that devours its own tail, symbolises the alchemical Mercury.

FATHER OF STONE: Alchemical Sulphur.

BIRD OF HERMES: Mythical volatile called Phenix, symbol of Mercury, synonymous with the Hermetic Cock and the Ansar.

PALACE: Another name for the Living Gold or Vitriol.

PALM DATE PALM: Philosopher's Stone RED.

DOVES OF DIANA: In the Régime of Mercury, they indicate the spiritualisation and fixation of the Mercury; in each sublimation they lose part of their feathers and make the Mercury more igneous.

The Doves of Diana is the most complicated enigma that must be untied in order to carry out the sublimations; it was devised by Irineo Filaleteo: "They are wrapped in the embraces of Venus". Fulcanelli clarifies that they go 2 parts of Dissolvent against one part of Venus".

PARABOLE: Greek word indicating an allegory, a symbol, an enigma, a comparison, or a story illustrative of the alchemical theme.

PARACELSUS, Theophaster: Swiss physician and alchemist of the 16th century, he attacked all the principles of the medical science of his time, making countless enemies, and developed a scientific method more than two centuries ahead of his contemporaries. He was assassinated and died with a shot in the forehead, although some modern researchers who have examined him refute this theory on the grounds that he was born with bone degeneration.

He is the author of numerous books on medicine, and has some dedicated to alchemy and magic; his works can be found in the National Library in Madrid (Spain):

- "Magic Archidoxia ".

- "The Treasury of Treasures".

- "Theory of Alchemy" (Works, 1894).

It should be noted that Theophrastus is an occultist much earlier than Paracelsus, and should not be confused with Paracelsus.

PART: Portion of something, element of a composition, place where...

PARTICULAR (SPAGIRICAL PROCEDURE): Spagyric procedure for obtaining gold from metals by methods close to alchemy.

The "Treatise on Azoth" by Basil Valentinus contains a Particular based on scientific alchemical principles, which has been described as exceptional.

PASSIVE: Subject that receives the catalytic action or chemical attack on another body. In alchemy it is the female of the mineral species that acts as a passive subject in the Great Work.

PAUWELS, Louis: French scientist and essayist who, working in collaboration with Jacques Bergier, edited the "Return of the Sorcerers" and "The Rebellion of the Sorcerers", which contain some references to alchemical matters.

PENTACLE: Five-pointed star, hieroglyph for the SUBJECT of art.

Let us clarify Fulcanelli's enigma by which the Alchemical Mercury follows the rules of the number 6, and which led Canseliet to know, erroneously, that it was antimony: Mercury is born from the pentacle, a five-pointed star, becoming the "mercury", represented by the six-pointed star or Solomon's seal, and then undergoes the seven Regimes, which lead it to the Philosophical Stone, represented by a seven-pointed star. The ruler reminds us of Ramon Lull with his tables.

CORASAN DOG (MALE): Black powder that is separated from the compound at the beginning of the work.

ARMENIA DOG (FEMALE): Appellative of the solvent.

PERNETTY, Don Antony Joseph: French monk, historian of Alchemy, lived in the 18th century and is the author of the "Dictionary of Hermetic Myth".

PERRENELLE: Name of Nicolas Flamel's wife, meaning "The Stone is in her".

PERSEUS: Son of Zeus and Danae who beheaded Medusa.

PHILALETES, Eirenaeus: See Irenaeus Philaletheus.

PHILOSOPHAL STONE: Objective sought by the alchemists, their aim is first to find it, then to perfect it and finally to apply it to the perfection of the three kingdoms of Nature.

PELARGOS: From the Greek PELOS (black) plus ARGOS (white), composed of black and white hides the airtight VESSEL made of black and white earth, white is the light that turns black.

WEIGHTS: Units

    tt - pound

    3 - ounce

    gr - grain

    gt - drop

    aa - equal parts

    gs - sufficient quantity

    Ms - handful

FISH: scaly animals that hide the materials of the work from the curious, and that live in the hermetic sea.

- blackish fish: first mercury

- boneless fish: the rising sulphur.

PILOT: alchemical sulphur, pilot of the living wave.

PYRITE: Ore of the mineral iron sulphide. In Greek it means "generator of fire".

PISON: Mythical river whose waters are composed of the four elements, it flows in the vessel through the Earth to which it gives life.

Name of an ancient philosopher.

STONES: Common designation for spagyric and alchemical products.

- Yellow Stone: Sulphur.

- White Stone: Silver transmuting stone.

- Cubic stone: Philosopher's stone.

- Fire Stone: Stone obtained with Antimony of great properties.

- Cornerstone: Philosopher's Stone.

- Black Magnet Stone: Daughter of Saturn.

- Red Stone: Transmuting stone of gold.

PLANETS: Each of the planets has a colour assigned to it, a metal it represents and a Regime in the Great Work; with an esoterically geocentric conception, the following planets are mentioned: Mercury, Venus, Mars, Jupiter, Saturn, the Moon and the Sun.

SILVER: Metal astrologically associated with the Moon, it is of great importance in jewellery, it is obtained alchemically, by the action of the White Stone.

- Living Silver: This is another name for commercial quicksilver, as well as alchemical Mercury, which Hortulanus defines as a matrix for receiving the sperm and the tincture of gold, with which it will cohabit for a long time. It is the hieroglyphic of Azoth and Alkaest.

POETRY: It comes from the Greek Poiesis, to make poems, verses. It also comes from the verb Poieo, to make, to manufacture, to build, to give birth.

POET: He is the maker, the builder of the Work, the practising Alchemist.

POISSON, Albert: Alchemist and sculptor of the end of the 19th century, he wrote:

- "Teories et simboles des Alchimistes", EdCharconac, Paris, 1891.

- "Cinq traites d'Alchimie", Ed. Charconac 1893.

POLE: From the Greek Polein, to turn around the pole, a point marked by the Pole Star which points to the North or the right path in the labyrinth of Alchemy. The star indicates the presence of a strong magnetic field which induces profound alterations within matter.

DUST OF PROJECTION: Stone used for transmutations.

CHICKEN: See rooster, of which it is a synonym.

PONTANO, Juan: 17th century Spanish alchemist, author of "Lapide Philosophico", Frankfurt 1614 and of "El Fuego Sófico".

FIRST AGENT: Secret Fire. Chaos of the Philosophers.

PROJECTION: Transmutation of a metal into GOLD or SILVER.

PUCHE RIART, J.A.: Contemporary author of technical books and books on Alchemy, among which we can highlight

among which we can highlight:

- "Synesius, roman alchemist" (alchemical novel).

- "The Revolution of the Alchemists".

- "The Alchemical Glossary".

- "Alchemy as seen by an Engineer".

He is the translator from French of:

- "The Treatise of the Azoth", by Basil Valentine.

- The Treatise on the Egg of the Philosophers, by Bernard of Treves.

PUTREFACCION: It comes from the Latin "putrefaction", in this operation the mixture becomes black, colour that appears in four points of the elaboration:

- In the first separation.
- In the first conjunction.

- At the second conjunction.

- At the fixation of the sulphur.

Quotations taken from Le Breton.

FIFTH ESSENCE: In Alchemy it is used to designate the Elixir, Universal Medicine and the Philosopher's Stone itself.

In Spagyrics, in addition to the designation used in Alchemy, it has numerous other names, it indicates any concentrated and pure essence, the central point of matter, around which the four elements revolve, the fifth being the quintessence, and also around which the seasons of the year revolve.

Quintessence requires that the body be stripped of superfluities and impurities by a very subtle and perfect distillation.

Any extract of very high concentration, or of great power, is called quintessence, and must always be composed in its administration of SALT, SULPHUR and MERCURY, which may be stored separately.

QUERMES: Prepared mercury.

RABELAIS, François: Pseudonym of Alcofribas Nassier, a 16th century French Benedictine monk, parish priest of Meudon, writer and teacher, he was one of the leading figures in the literature of the neighbouring country.

In his well-known works he uses a descriptive system based on the knowledge of the authors, and of the ancient Greek, Roman and Hebrew languages, to conceal the technology of alchemy by cabalistic methods of language; in the very title of Gargantua he calls himself an "extractor of quintessence", i.e. an alchemist.

To understand is copied by Swift in Gulliver's Travels, leaving the knowledge of its author in the expressions and names, so strange to those who have not studied this science, as Eugène Canseliet demonstrates.

Another well-known work is the History of the giant "Pantagruel".

ROOT: It comes from the Latin Radix. It indicates the origin, the beginning and the prime matter of the Great Work.

RASES: 10th century Arab alchemist.

REBIS: From the Latin RE (two times) BIS (things), synonymous with the androgynous. It is the sublimated Mercury or Azoth.

RECIPE: From the Latin Recipe, take, spagyric or alchemical procedure for the manufacture of medicines; also spagyric particulars, and finally any formula for producing a chemical reaction.

CONTAINER: Vessel or canister capable of containing solids or liquids.

NET = SUTILE: The one that appears when the Mercury is obtained, on its surface.

REGIME: The phases that the Mercury undergoes during the accomplishment of the Great Work. Each of them contains several others; Philalete defines seven, with the names of the Planets.

The Regime of Fire is the manner of carrying the furnace, increasing it very gradually as the Work progresses, passing from spring, to autumn, and finally the hot summer; this secret has been very jealously guarded by the alchemists of all ages.

- Mercury Regime: First of the work, by means of the "labours of Hercules" the materials are processed, the SALT, SULPHUR and MERCURY are obtained, and from them the Regimen culminates with the obtaining of the AZOTH, the only one of the Great Work. It is done in SPRING.

- Saturnian Regime: First to undergo REBIS, it is characterised by the BLACK colour and the cadaverous odour of matter.

- Jupiter Regime: Regime following that of Saturn, the matter becomes clearer and takes on an ashen grey colour, similar to that of chestnut. The smell is more pleasant.

- Moon Regime: Following the Jupiter Regime, the matter takes on a capillary appearance and a very white colour and capillary appearance predominates, starting at the periphery, with the lunar GROWTH, and progressing along the Regime, reaching the whole vessel, arriving at the FULL MOON. From this Regimen the first alchemical medicine is extracted.

- Venus Regime: This Regime follows the Moon Regime, and is characterised by the colours of the Peacock's tail, which range from bright red to emerald green, varying continuously throughout the Regime.

- Mars Regime: Following the Venus Régime comes the Mars Régime, characterised by orange and reddish colours and the smell of ether.

- Sun Regime: The last Regime of the Stone, which very few alchemists have known, is characterised by a very fragrant odour and the reddish-garnet colour of the walls of the vessel, as well as the fluidity of the Stone.

RULE: In Latin Regir, to govern the fire in accordance with the Regimen, a rule that must be scrupulously followed.

To rule correctly, it is necessary to know the degrees of fire, which, according to Diego de Torres Villaroel, are:

- 1st degree: Placing the hand in the oven, in the ashes, does not produce any injury known to burn.

- 2nd degree: The hand can withstand the heat of the oven and no more.

- 3rd degree: coals are added and the fire is fortified.

- 4th degree: fire in flame and holm oak wood.

STARBURNING MARTIAL REGULA: According to Lemery and Basil Valentin, it must be prepared from stibnite with iron filings and tartar from the barrels, in the proportions indicated. The second and third fusions do not require "Martian" filings.

Regulus means Little King, little king, an appellative given to compounds in which the STAR appears. They can be made with lead, antimony and arsenic.

REINCRUDING: Equivalent to recrudesce, to make a metal crude again, consisting of the addition of a certain substance to the metal in a state of fusion, so that it returns to its original state, retrograding the metal to its original juvenile state.

KINGDOMS: Those of Nature. Animal, Vegetable and Mineral. Regimes.

LITTLE KING: Alchemical sulphur. See Regulus.

RETORT: Vessel usually made of thick glass, and formerly of stoneware, nowadays not found, with a neck in the shape of a horn inclined downwards, which has earned it the nickname of horned, especially in the country of Gaul.

REVERB: The reverberatory furnace is indispensable for the realisation of the whole Work, the flame circulates and returns from above on the material; if the athanor has no passage through the top, the furnace is of complete reverberation, and if it is open at the back and the sides are closed, the circulation is only half-circulation.

RIPLEY, George: 15th century English alchemist, author of the "Twelve Doors", Opera Omnia Chemica, 1694.

ROCK: Synonym of Philosopher's Stone.

OAK: French hieroglyphic for the first material as extracted from the ore. In English the correct translation is ENCINA.

DEW: From the Latin Roris, lustral water that in springtime floods the meadows before dawn. The alchemical dew is produced in the interior of the RETORTA and is a derivative of SULPHUR; it is indispensable to the Work as its SOUL. Its hieroglyph is the rose, which in Latin Rosa, in the tense rosis, links directly with roris, genitive of ros, dew.

HERMETIC ROSE: Fruit of Alchemy. Roses are always picked with thorns, according to the Rosicrucians.

ROSICRUCIAN: Synonym of Alchemist, Knight of the Rocco Cocido according to Fulcanelli. The best known Rosicrucian Texts are the Fama Fraternitatis, the Confession and the Chemical Wedding of Rosenkreutz.

RED: Hieroglyphic colour of the secret fire of the Alchemists. Hieroglyphic of the 3rd Matter.

ROSENKREUTZ, Christian: Pseudonym of Valentin Andrade, disciple of Philaletetus and teacher of St. Germain, writes "The Chemical Wedding" (Ed. 7 1/2 Esoteric Library).

CELESTIAL RUBI: Name given by Irenaeus Philaleteus to the Philosopher's Stone in his treatise, a brief guide to the Celestial Ruby.

RUBIFY: From the Latin Rubificatio, to redden, to turn a ruby or thyrsus colour.

WHEEL: Fire of. The path of multiplication of the Stone, repeating the regimes, beginning with that of Mercury and ending with that of the Sun.

WISDOM: Applies to the complete and detailed knowledge of the compounds and operations throughout the complicated process of Alchemy.

SAGE: Master Alchemist has obtained by his means the Stone by the principal means; the dry or the wet.

SACRAMENTUM: From the Latin sacramentum, ferment, leaven. See ferment.

SAINT GERMAIN: Alchemist and diplomat of the 18th century, of a very disturbing history, the date of his death is not known, and he appears on numerous occasions, the last of which is said to have appeared before the cameras of TVE in a popular programme in which he performed a public and videotaped transmutation. He is the author of the "Holy Trinity", translated by Ed. 7 1/2 Esoteric Library.

SALT: One of the components of the vessel. According to Paracelsus the three components are Sulphur, Mercury and Salt.

Every body reduced to ashes shows its SALT. By bringing together Salt, Sulphur and Mercury, the whole body can be restored (Basil Valentin).

SALAMANDER: Central Salt that lives in fire, feeds on fire and is coloured throughout the whole Work.

Salt is found even in the ASH of metals, which the ancients called METALLIC SEED.

The sols are extracted by LIXIVATION in all processes and in Alchemy require the knowledge of the Secret Fire: Remember the Salamander to defeat the DRAGON.

SALMON Guillaume: Alchemist famous for being the author of the "Library of the Chemical Philosophers" Paris, 1672.

SALPETRE: In French it is called salpêtre, salt of the stone, in Spagyric it is potassium nitrate, NO_3K.

SATURN: Hieroglyphic of the first matter of the alchemists and name of the 2nd Regime of the Stone.

In spagyrics it is Lead. In mineral theophony it is represented by Saint Saturn, one of the patrons of Soria.

VEGETAL SATURNIA: Mercury after the first conjunction, green in colour. Vegetable" stone or first state of the Stone.

SCHMIEDER, Karl Christoph: German professor of the 19th century, profound researcher of the history of Alchemy, published an extraordinary book of pleasant reading: "Geschite der Alchimie", Halle 1832.

SEQUENCES OF COLOUR: The order in which the colours appear in the Great Work, they are collected in the Mutus Liber, in an orderly sequence. Frequency which corresponds to that of the development of the Seven Regimes.

SEGANISSEDE: Genius of the Sages of the Abandoned Word, Alchemical Mercury.

MAGICAL SEAL OF HERMES: It is the famous seal of Solomon and the Star of David, the star that guides the alchemist to the beginning of the Great Work. In Spagyrics, it is also understood as the hermetic lute of a vessel.

SEED: Metals preserve the seed in their ashes, as it is incombustible.

SHEFELD: 18th century Austrian alchemist.

SENDOVINGIUS, Michael: A Moravian alchemist of the 17th century, heir of the Cosmopolitan, whom he helped to escape from the prison in which he was imprisoned, and who later married his widow. He compiled the latter's works, understood them and subsequently published the treatise "Nova Lumen Chimicum" 1650.

SEPARATORY, Art of: Spagyric art of the decomposition of a body into its principles, in order to then reunite them in the proportions suitable for the purposes of chemistry. Spagyrics is based on this art.

SERMONISHING: From the Latin Sermoneo, it means blowing, insufflation. It is also in fact applied by some spagyrics to the effects of the excessive ingestion of drinks rich in the spirit of wine, and to the unscientific sayings of blowers, who fill hearts with false hopes.

SNAKE-SERPENT: Name of Mercury which, when "opened" presents a scaly appearance like the skin of a snake, is poisonous. The AZOTH is the snake that bites its own tail, the OUROBOROS.

SERPENTINE: Greenish colour of a snake, which takes the Alchemical Source. Colour of the mineral Serpentine tending to black.

SETHON, Alexander: Name of the cosmopolitan, author of the "Philosophical Letter".

SYBILES: Mythological characters of female sex, who, according to the Greeks, were the three Harpies, followers of the Hermetic Philosophy, and of great cruelty.

One of the SYBILAS was Medusa.

SIGN: The Star of David, which appears in the conjunction, confirming the union of Heaven and earth, is the proof of the alchemical CONCEPTION.

SIMPLES: Simple, pure substances, indecomposable elements.

SYMPTOM: Indication, sign, warning of a chemical reaction, observable chemical effect, such as an oenolic change when two wines are mixed.

SINGULAR: From the Latin Singularis, a simple, simple method for obtaining a chemical compound. Another appellation of the spagyric Particulars.

SYRENE: Hieroglyph for the alchemical SULPHUR.

SOPHISTIC: From the Latin Sophisto, chatty, applied to useless procedures; sophists are called sophists.

SUN: Planetary name for gold, which in Greek is Helios and in Hebrew is Jes, which is why Jesus the Nazarene of the house of Jesse was of a SOLAR house and of alchemists.

The sun designates the metal Gold, the Philosophical Gold and the Astral Gold.

SOLVE ET COAGULA: Latin words that summarise all the operations of the magisterium, as Irenaeus says "dissolve the fixed, volatilise the dissolved, and then fix it into powder".

The philosophical SOLUTION is distinguished from chemical solutions in that the SOLVENT does not assimilate the basic metal offered to it, it rejects its molecules and breaks their cohesion, taking over the fragments of SULPHUR contained in the metal, leaving the residue sterile, disintegrated and completely irreducible.

The solution of the SALT of RED BRASS is obtained by leaching, with the help of the spirit of GREEN BRASS, with great patience, reiterating the affusion of the spirit on the body, for a long time.

SOLUTION: Spagyric operation consisting in the introduction into an aqueous substance of another solid and dry substance, which by this method becomes liquid.

SPINOZA, Baruch: 17th century Dutch alchemist.

SPIRITUS MUNDII: Spirit of the world, SULPHUR.

STARKEY, George: 17th century English pharmacist, he met Philaletius in America, when he saw him perform a transmutation in his house; when he asked the alchemist for information, he denied it, claiming that only God granted it to those who deserved it. In the National Library of Madrid, the works of Philaletheus appear as attributed to this man, as well as those of Eugene Philaletheus.

TARTAR: Cremor tartar, potassium tartar obtained from barrels, in its crudest state, for chemists.

For the Spagyrists, Tartarus can mean the "little hell" in which the reacting elements are made to suffer the torture of fire, in the manner of Purgatory.

In Alchemy it is used as a hieroglyphic symbol of the first material of the work, which is extracted from the "OAK", just as tartarus is extracted from the barrel of oak.

TELESMA: From the Greek Telos, death, used to indicate the black colour, a symptom of putrefaction, hieroglyphic of the Raven.

HERMETIC TEMPEST: Storm that occurs in the ALUDEL when the SULPHUR is born including the swell that rocks the hermetic vessel.

THEION: Greek word meaning divine, pointing to Sulphur and the Red Lion.

MINERAL THEOPHANY: The study of Alchemy in the light of texts and Religious buildings, in any religion.

TIME: Each Regime requires a time to be executed, which cannot be shortened.

EARTH: One of the four elements. It is represented as follows:

- Fetid Earth: Earth of a black colour, of a fetid "smell".

- Condemned Earth: Moszakumia.

- Roman Earth: Amalgam of sublimations, with an earthy appearance, also known as "wise man's earth" or philosophical earth, as it resembles the reddish clay of an apothecary.

TIFFEREAU: 19th century spagyric alchemist.

DYEING: With the ability to dye metals into gold, silver or another metal G. Colouring agent.

THYRIUM: Purple in colour.

TOLLIUS, J: Author of "Le Chemin du Ciel Chimique".

TONEL: The holm oak barrel represents the 1st MATTER used by the alchemists. The OAK is the hieroglyph that hides the SUBJECT of ART.

TOWER: Hieroglyph for the third matter, the mineral, which is the envelope, the refuge, the protective asylum of the mercurial DRAGON.

TRANSFIGURATE: Changes of colour that appear in a determined sequence, like a magic lantern, throughout the different Regimes.

TRANSMUTATION: Alchemical transformation of one metal into another.

TREATY OF NATURE: A work of the Cosmopolitan.

TRITURATION: From the Latin triturare, crushing of a substance until it is "calcined".

TURBA: From the Latin Turba, assembly, compilation of ancient Philosophers. Denomination of a Work of Alchemy; The "Turba Philosopharum", assembly of the Disciples of Pythagoras, called the Code of Truth, Salmon Vol II.

UNITY: All one, inseparable union of the three Principles that compose the Stone.

Name of an ancient alchemical treatise: "Treatise on Unity".

Unity of Chaos, and Mystery of the Trinity in the Mineral Theophany.

URBIGERUS, Baro: Author of "One Hundred Aphorisms" 1690.

VAN HELMONT, John Baptist: 17th century physician and chemist, author of "L'Aurore de la Medicine", Amsterdam, 1648.

VAUGHAN (VAGAN), Thomas: Name of Eugenio Filaleteo, whose works are in the National Library in Madrid, confused with those of Irineo Filaleteo in the pseudonym of George Starkey.

VESSELS: The name given to the vessel and its contents in any of the alchemical processes.

The vessel should be of CLEAR and TRANSPARENT glass, without blisters or bubbles, and of sufficient strength.

WAND OF GOLD: Alchemical sulphur.

VENUS: Planet which in Spagyrics points to copper and in Alchemy to Sulphur. The Régime of Venus is the Fifth of the Great Work. Hieroglyphic of alchemical sulphur and of the matter from which it is obtained, of which we know that it is almost all DYE, doomed to perish with it, unless accompanied by a fixed body in which it can establish its seat and abode in a stable and permanent manner.

VERIDICUS: From the Latin Veridicus, which speaks the truth, it is used to incline the student to the obligation of the accomplishment of the wet way, longer and dearer to the alchemists.

WAY: Path. The alchemist follows them to obtain the Philosopher's Stone. The wet way can be divided into two others, one shorter than the other. The dry path is unique.

The wet path is the ONLY one that allows the attainment of the AZOTH, three matters and only one way. From the Azoth, one can take the wet way or the dry way.

In Spagyrics, the use of BRIEF ways has been much sought after, as obtaining quintessences can be very laborious. Raimundo Lulio shows the student a BRIEF procedure for the extraction of quintessences in his "Libro de los Secretos de la Naturaleza o quinta-esencia", Ed. Doble R.

TRAVELLER: Pilgrim. Mercury.

VIATIC: Use in extremis of Universal Medicine.

The use of this medicine produced the rapid cure of a sick man of Paracelsus, who did not want to pay him, leading him to various lawsuits.

WIND: Volatile spirit, air. Our mercury.

VINEGAR: Very sour liquor extracted from sulphur. Red Mercury.

WHITE VIRGINS: Images of the Virgin of the Milk, of purely Alchemical significance, i.e: the one in the Monastery of Oseira, a few kilometres from Lugo (Spain).

BLACK VIRGINS: Images of the Virgo Parituri, who is to be a mother. Many of them are ancient statuettes of Isis; even though they are relatively few and without exception they are full of votive offerings. Ceres and Cybele are synonyms of Isis.

VITRIOL: The solvent of the Alchemists, according to Basil Valentinus. According to Fulcanelli it is sulphur: Vit means life; R is air, one of the alchemical catalysts; OL is kabalistically close to OR, gold, and is therefore considered the Living Gold. A third non-alchemist type, such as Cyliani, defines the following evolution of the word: Vitriol --> Glass --> Crystal, an anagram of the Salt of Christ or Sal Harmoniaco.

Basil defends that the word is: Visita Interiore Terrae, Rectictiphicando Invenies Ocultum Lapidam: Visit the Interior of the Earth, Rectictiphicando Invenies Ocultum Lapidam: Visit the Interior of the Earth, rectifying you will reach the Hidden Stone.

In Spagyricon it means oil.

VIVIFY: Action of the Alkaest which re-incrudes metals, breathing life and Youth into them. See REINCRUDE.

ARIES WOMB: According to the Antimonists it is the "foetus" extracted from the dew after the Athanor's productive gestation, which is forty days in absolute darkness.

VOLATILE: Birds are volatile because they are able to take flight and fly away, and the same can happen with a substance, deposited in an open vessel, and on going to use it, find it empty-handed; this volatilisation can be caused by the action of fire, and occurs with solids as well as liquids, the cases which are best known to the public are those of iodine and of alcohol or water, which soon dry up.

In Alchemy, birds or volatiles are hieroglyphs of mercury.

VULGAR: From the Latin Vulgare, from the public domain. It is one of the fires used in Alchemy.

- W -

WIRTH, Oswald: Author contemporary of "Le Tarot des Imaginiers du Moyen Age" Ed. Tchou. 1966.

YGE, Claude D': Contemporary author, "La Nouvelle assemblée des Philosophes chymiques", Derby Libres, Paris, 1954.

YAVE: Name of God, hides the minerals involved in the great work through the acronym (iod he vau he).

ZACHAIRE, Denis: 16th century French alchemist, author of "L'Opuscule de la Philosophie des Metaux", Salmon Vol II.

ZEUS: Father of PERSEUS. Mythological god of all the gods.

FOX (female): The Alchemical Mercury, symbolised by the Rooster, must become the PHOENIX, but first it must reach a state of provisional FIXITY, symbolised by the FOX, the dry water acquires a saline consistency when the procedure for retaining it for a long time in the fire is discovered, and thus resists a temperature that would be sufficient to evaporate it in its entirety in its previous state. This situation is temporary, because it is re-dissolved in the WATER from which it was born in order to give it back its volatility with the complexion, wings and tail of the ROOK.

ZOSIMUS, The Panapolitan: Alchemist of the 3rd or 4th century, born in Alexandria, author of the Treatise on Virtue and the Treatise on Furnaces.

YGE, Claude D': Contemporary author, "La Nouvelle assemblée des Philosophes chymiques", Derby Libres, Paris, 1954.

YAVE: Name of God, hides the minerals involved in the great work through the acronym (iod he vau he).

Printed in Great Britain
by Amazon

10072991R00088